AF662839

Presented To:

From:

Date:

JUMPSTART *your* MOTIVATION

JUMPSTART *your* MOTIVATION

—10 JOLTS—
TO GET MOTIVATED
AND STAY MOTIVATED

SHAWN DOYLE

EBD
EMBASSY BOOKS
www.embassybooks.in

© Copyright 2011—Shawn Doyle

First published in India 2012.

All rights reserved. This book is protected by the copyright laws of the United States of America. This book may not be copied or reprinted for commercial gain or profit. The use of short quotations or occasional page copying for personal or group study is permitted and encouraged. Permission may be granted upon request.

Published in India by :
Embassy Book Distributors,
Great Western Building,
Maharashtra Chamber of Commerce Lane,
Kala Ghoda, Fort,
Mumbai - 400 023.

Email : info@embassybooks.in
Website : www.embassybooks.in

ISBN : 978-93-81860-19-9

Printed in India by Repro India Ltd., Mumbai

ENDORSEMENTS

Finally we have a book on motivation that gets people off the couch and into action!! Shawn Doyle has masterfully written the ultimate book on Motivation. It should be entitled, "How to Get Unstuck, Achieve Anything, and Live Your Life!" Shawn provides concrete action steps and exactly-how-to strategies to motivate yourself and lead others to greater levels of inspired performance. You deserve this book now so you can act upon your dreams and live a powerful life!

STEVEN ROWELL

The IDEA Doctor™, Author, *Clean Is Not Enough!*

Founder, Reconnect Consulting and Abundance Publishing

Shawn Doyle's *Jumpstart Your Motivation* is a must read for anyone wanting to become a "Continuous Non-Stop Learning Machine" (Foundation #3). Shawn's to-the-point, fun, and creative style of writing makes it easy for anyone understand and put into everyday practical use.

KIM WOODWORTH

Regional VP, Comcast Spotlight

As a publisher of a regional business to business publication in Pennsylvania, I've had the pleasure of dealing with Shawn both on a personal level as well as publishing his monthly leadership column. Reading *Jumpstart Your Motivation* has only solidified my respect for his high-caliber content. Shawn's "foundations" should really be labeled principles for business leaders to live by. He offers a balanced approach that can be easily adopted by anybody wanting to improve their professional *and* personal lives.

STEVE SCHULZ
Publisher, *Business2Business* magazines

Jumpstart Your Motivation will leap you into action! This handy guide gave practical and tangible tools for kick-starting me into movement. Shawn Doyle is a master at driving you to align your personal and professional passions for ultimate achievement.

DINA WEINBERG
CEO and Founder, MindLight Global

This easy-to-read book is loaded with powerful and useful strategies everyone will find valuable.

LAWRENCE ELEFTHERI
VP, Central Division, Charter Media

I've read many books on motivation, but Shawn's *Jumpstart Your Motivation* is my favorite. It's a quick read, concise, and full of great information that I can use on a daily basis. And...it fits conveniently in my briefcase. Who could ask for anything more?

PATSY GINSBERG

Jumpstart Your Motivation is a concise, well-written, and easy to follow guide I would recommend to anyone who wants to stay on track with all aspects of their professional and personal lives.

ALISON FARN LEIGH

Grounded in real-world practicality, this is my favorite resource for staying motivated and on-track. My copy is well worn.

TERRY MARRAN
Director, Debit and EBT Compliance, First Data

This book is one of the most practical, relevant tools on motivation available on the market today. Shawn has a unique ability to challenge the reader to apply his recommendations immediately. A fabulous combination of stories, suggestions, examples, and interactive WORKIT section makes this a valuable resource for individuals or companies wanting to achieve more. This is more than a book, it is a road-map for a new mindset—*Jumpstart Your Motivation* is a must-read and must-apply strategy.

NEEN JAMES
International Productivity Expert
Neen James Communications

This book is a gold mine. It offers key strategies and personal insights that you can use to have greater success and happiness in every part of your life.

MARY BETH FORD
Author of *Wisdom from the Gardens: Life Lessons*

I was so motivated after reading this book and doing the exercises that I gave a copy to my franchisor, John Hewitt— he is always looking for great books! He was inspired by it as well, and immediately sent a copy to every franchisee and corporate employee in our company!

DAWN S. FILETTI
Enrolled Agent-President of Chesco Tax, Inc. T/A Liberty Tax Service

This dense and rich resource is tops. Rather than re-hash trite concepts, Shawn packs a ton of fresh and thought-provoking concepts and "recipes" into a user-friendly format. Equally applicable to all comers, the content and calls to action are stimulating and genuinely motivating. As in all that Shawn does, it stands high above the rest.

BRADLEY P. CASEMORE
MHSA, MSW, CHE-President, Bracing Futures, Inc.

This book is the best kick in the pants you'll ever get. If you read them and take action, you're holding 100 simple pages that will change your life

KATE ZABRISKIE
CEO and Founder, Business Training Works Inc.

Anyone who reads this book can apply the knowledge for immediate results in their lives. It has helped my business become more successful.

SCOTT A. JEFFERYS
Managing Partner, Jefferys & Associates, P.C.

While I believe that life should be a great journey, my path is often obscured by the mundane details of everyday existence. Jumpstart Your Motivation not only helps me to see above and beyond the daily commotion, it also charges me with the enthusiasm needed to take great steps down my path today!

CURTIS JURGENSON
Senior Account Executive, Givaudan Fragrances Corp

Motivation is a fundamental building block of success in any sales organization, and Shawn's book provides great insight into this difficult to manage component of the business. Shawn has helped our sales team capture and uncover the power of motivation.

DEREK HANSON
Div. VP, West/Mid-West, Charter Media

At first you may think that you'll give this book a quick look, after all, it is pretty thin in terms of pages. Be advised, this may be the toughest excursion into motivation that you'll ever embark upon. If you apply the advice and techniques provided by Shawn Doyle, you just might be surprised at what you're able to accomplish.

ROBERT D SLAUTER
Regional Training Manager, Office Depot

Jumpstart Your Motivation is easy to follow, practical & fun. The book is great because it doubles as a workbook with spaces for writing down your responses. It is a must-have to move you to the next level.

KIMBERLY HALL
President Chester County Historical Society

This was one of the most influential career-enrichment resources I have had the opportunity and pleasure to experience, and has had quite a positive effect on my own personal career as well as all of my associates.

DANA LAROSSA
President-CEO, LaRossa Consulting Group

Shawn's book is a treasury of motivational insights. His humorous and enlightened stories contain strong action points that inspire people to take positive action to better their lives. I heartily recommend his book!

MIKE GURNICZ
CEO, The Synergy Club

Shawn Doyle's book, Jumpstart Your Motivation has great "can do" information and techniques that really work! We have seen this put to practice with several clients and many attendees, all with great results. We constantly await his next book.

LAUREN ANDERSON
CEO, Lauren Anderson Associates, Inc.

Jumpstart Your Motivation blew me away. I loved every minute of it, and I recommend it to my clients on a daily basis. Shawn has a way of making everyone feel that they can accomplish their goals if they work smart to attain them! He is captivating, motivating, and nothing less than spectacular.

JOE SPIVAK
President, Onsite Training Partners, Inc

Shawn Doyle has a gift for teaching motivation, one of the greatest necessities for achieving success. If you want to learn how to become successful and stay motivated, then this book is a must.

JERRY JOHNSON
Director, The Apologetics Group

I picked up Shawn's book when it was first published and couldn't put it down until I had read it the entire book! I found it masterfully done: truly inspirational and practical at the same time. His book has helped me to become and remain fully motivated toward achieving my personal and professional dreams and goals. Thank you Shawn!

BILL BELKNAP
Founder, PAH Learning Center
Manager, Operations, Pfizer Animal Health

I used to watch other people climb the ladder to the top. *Jumpstart Your Motivation* helped me to rise above them. I am still soaring!

CARRIE WIMER

Incisive—that's the word that our executive readers use to evaluate Shawn Doyle's contributions to Business2Business Magazines. Shawn has an authentic voice that resonates with real-world business practitioners.

TED BYRNE

Managing Editor/Economist, Business2Business Publications

Most people believe books on motivation relate to only their workmates or employees, but Shawn's Jumpstart Your Motivation makes you realize that it applies to you as well. Shawn shows how anyone can be perpetually motivated.

STEVEN BOSTICK

Supervisor of Distribution Operations

United States Postal Service

I found the content SOLID! This is a great book! I recommend it as a solid "Foundation" for anyone experiencing life!

PETER S. (PETE) HEGEDUS

Principal, Independence International Associates

DEDICATION

THIS book is dedicated to the following people:

My wife Cindy, the light and love of my life, my constant and ever present inspiration, thank you for being my friend, advisor, and cheerleader. You always believed in me. You are and will always be special.

My daughter, Alexis; who is a daily inspiration the smartest and the funniest person on the planet. You are a bright light that draws people in to you.

My Mom and Dad; for raising me in a positive environment; for teaching me that all things are possible. I am lucky to be your son.

My brother, Larry, and sister, Traci; for being the best brother and sister in the world.

Filemon Lopez, the best leader I have ever worked for and with. You are an amazing person and had a personal and professional impact you will never comprehend.

Harland Model, for being an outstanding mentor and friend and for showing me the meaning of grace.

Bob Slauter, for being a great sounding board, advisor, and friend in times of dark and light.

Dave Gregory, for being there as a best friend, advisor, and great source of inspiration, humor and encouragement at all times. You are the best.

Paul O'Keefe for being a great mentor, business advisor, and friend.

Steve Bostick, for the constant flow of great ideas, enthusiasm, and encouragement.

I am truly honored to call you all friends.

CHAPTER ONE

THE FIRST GIANT STEP

"Let us then be up and doing,
With a heart for any fate,
Still achieving still pursuing,
Learn to labor and to wait."

—H.W. LONGFELLOW
A Psalm of Life

I would like to thank you for the courageous act of picking up this book. Wanting to learn is the first giant step in getting motivated and staying motivated. Wanting to be motivated is the first step in being motivated. You have taken the first giant step. I congratulate you for that. I wrote this book for you because I want to help you in any way I can. This book is written for you.

I am not a doctor (and I don't play one on T.V.). I am not a psychiatrist or psychologist. I am not an "expert." I am a member of the human race just like you. I don't have all the answers. I have read about and studied human motivation all my life. I have trained thousands of people in the last fifteen years in the U.S., Canada, and England. I am fascinated by one aspect of training; I have found that many times the training inspires and motivates people. I find that to be an honor, but also somewhat puzzling. Why do I motivate them? Why does the training motivate them? What had they not heard before they took the class? Why weren't they motivated before? Why are some people less motivated than others? What are the elements that make someone more or less motivated?

After the completion of a training session, a man about 55 years old came over to shake my hand. He was visibly moved, with tears in his eyes. He shook my hand and said, "I want to thank you, this session changed me."

I asked him why, and he said he had been in a rut for a long time and now he wasn't. He was out of his rut and fully energized. This experience was deeply gratifying for me on a professional and personal level, and yet something bothered me. Several weeks later it hit me: How was this man going to keep from going back into a rut at some point? I had not given him that. I had only given him a temporary boost.

That was the thought that lead me to write this book. I believe that, through this book, I can give people some specific tools—tools to help them not only *get* motivated but *stay* motivated.

In this book, I will provide practical, useful tools and techniques to get motivated and stay motivated, and to help you achieve the goals that will maximize your life both personally and professionally. I want you to be a person who is FIRED

UP! I can give you information, but it is up to you to truly apply it to your life.

I can take you to the water but I can't make you drink. The biggest personal thrill for me would be to have made a small difference in your life. So... get ready to drink!

PEOPLE ARE LIKE GOLF BALLS.

I think that people are a lot like golf balls. Yes, I said golf balls. I would like for you to sit back and think a minute about a little golf ball. Technically, this little white ball is a round object made from a core of rubber, some rubber bands, and a plastic cover. As a young boy, I used to sit in the yard and cut away the cover of a golf ball with a pocketknife to try to uncover the mystery of the golf ball's power. I was disappointed to discover that the ball inside was a mass of bands and nothing more.

A golf ball when hit by me (the non-golfer) will travel maybe ten yards. But in the hands of an expert golfer, it has the potential to travel an amazing 250 yards!

What does a golf ball have to do with human potential and motivation? Everything! I think that, like golf balls, each one of us has unlimited potential. Assuming that you have most of your faculties, we all have pretty much the same biological makeup. We all have brains, hearts, and emotions. All of us are made of (more or less) the same material. We all have the ability to think. So why do some people fly high and others only dribble along? Why do some people succeed while others fail miserably? In my opinion, there is one compelling difference, and that is motivation. Motivation is the key performance differential. It is the fire in the belly of the stove.

Before you react in a negative way to the positive mental attitude, pie in the sky, book selling, motivational seminar, audio lesson, back slapping cliché, give this message a chance. Please open your mind for the moment if you want to see a change in your life.

Sadly, in this nation, I think that the word motivation has been given a bad name. I suspect that part of the reason is some of the speakers who travel the country doing motivational seminars. I find that most of them have a great message—but the problem with some is that they seem very insincere, and they don't seem like they really mean what they say. Most people have a built-in sensor that picks up on a lack of sincerity.

The other reason motivation has been given a bad name is that the negative people of the world just cannot stand for others to be positive—it is their goal to drag you down screaming into the abyss with them. They want to shoot you down; they have been put on the earth to drag you down with them. They do *not* want you to be positive!

Try this experiment one day to see how people react. On a Monday, go to work and wait for someone to ask you about your weekend. Look them in the eye and say

"It was great! I read a wonderful book by ________," (insert name of any motivational speaker) Now watch the reaction. They will probably frown and say something like, "Oh *that* guy? He is weird."

Or they will say, "Oh, *her*?" and roll their eyes.

When given a chance, most people will shoot a positive message down. Why? Because we live in a world where there are negative people breeding, having, and raising negative kids who have *more* negative kids. The cycle continues (watch the Jerry Springer show some day.) We now have colonies of negative people on the planet. Negative thinking is like a cancer that spreads rapidly. Just watch the evening news sometime. (Then again, I would advise against it—it's a real downer!)

YOU ARE A HIGH PERFORMANCE ENGINE

I want you to think of yourself as a high performance engine. Food is your biological fuel, but what fuels the rest of you? What keeps you going inside your brain and your heart? Motivation is your mental fuel, and if you want to be the very best, staying motivated will drive your success. Because you are a high performance engine, you also need to be very careful about what you put into your "tank." Your brain is a highly sophisticated mechanism that responds to the stimulus that is provided, whether it is positive or very negative.

Many studies have shown that watching a grisly murder scene in a horror movie or in real life is no different to your subconscious mind. So you must be very careful as to how you are "fueling" your high performance engine. It will only perform to the quality of the level of the fuel that is provided.

In this book I will share with you the *10 Foundations of Motivation*. They are simple and easy to read, but will take work and energy to put them into practice. None of them are rocket science.

Here are the foundations that will be covered in each chapter:

FOUNDATION #1
HAVE A PURPOSE FOR WHAT YOU DO

Kenneth Hilderbrandt said, "Strong lives are motivated by dynamic purposes."

Do you know your purpose? I am sure at this point you are saying, "That's easy—I go to work because I get paid, and my purpose is to get paid." Well, in my opinion, that is a reason not a purpose. I would venture to say that most people don't have a purpose and have no idea why they are doing what they are doing!

I want you to start to thinking about your life and career and define your true purpose. This is *your* life after all, and you don't just want to go through the motions! Another way to evaluate your purpose is to consider questions, such as:

"Why are you where you are?" and "What were you truly meant to do?" Having a true purpose and knowing what it is will be the rocket fuel to get motivated and help you stay motivated!

FOUNDATION #2
HAVE A PASSION FOR WHAT YOU DO

Have you ever met someone who is passionate about what they do? Is Tiger Woods passionate about golf? Is Richard Simmons passionate about exercise? Was Mother Teresa passionate about helping others? Is Bruce Springsteen passionate about music?

I think Sheila Graham said it best: "You can have anything you want if you want it desperately enough. You must want it with an inner exuberance that erupts through the skin and joins the energy created by the world."

If you aren't passionate about anything, in my opinion it is because either you haven't found your passion, or you had a passion that you gave up on many years ago. If that is the case, I think that is just plain sad. I have known many people in the past who have told me stories about their one passion, and how they gave it up due to circumstances in their life.

Unfortunately, there are many people walking this planet who do not have any passion about what they do. They live lives that are very mundane and boring. They have given up on their dreams, or as Henry David Thoreau said, they are "living lives of quiet desperation." I believe that passion is the energy that drives excellence and superior results.

FOUNDATION #3
BE A CONTINUOUS NON-STOP EARNING MACHINE

To quote Bob Perlman, "Learning is what most adults will do for a living in the 21st century."

Many people graduate from high school and college and they seem to say, "Okay, I'm done." Wrong!

They feel like they are finished and they stop reading, stop studying, and, in essence, they stop growing. I know many people who haven't read a book since school! Every year, you must be willing to reinvent yourself.

Because the shelf life of knowledge is so short in our society, the knowledge you graduate with doesn't last very long. Reading and continuous learning will separate you from most of the rest of society. You will perform better and grow in your professional and personal life—and that is very motivating.

FOUNDATION #4
BE A MENTOR AND HAVE A MENTOR

Mentoring is a classic case of two heads being better than one. In the words of George Bernard Shaw, "The only service a friend can render is to keep up your courage by holding up to you a mirror in which you can see a noble image of yourself."

When you have a mentor, it is very motivating because they are motivated by helping you get to the next level. They help you see the world through different glasses. When you are a mentor, you learn more about yourself, and it can be very motivating to see your protégé succeed.

FOUNDATION #5
KNOW WHAT GETS YOU MOTIVATED AND STIMULATED

Reggie Leach once said, "Success is not the result of spontaneous combustion. You must set yourself on fire." In other words, you really must know what it is that gets you pumped and "fired up."

I have movies, inspirational books, and certain music or activities that help me stay fired up. You need to experiment and know what gets you in the state of high motivation. Once you have identified these tools, use them when you have had a bad day to provide the motivational kick that you need.

FOUNDATION #6
REWARD YOURSELF FOR ACHIEVING

> *"Call it what you will, incentives are what get people to work harder."*
>
> —Nikita Khrushchev

When you set goals, and you achieve them, it is absolutely essential to reward yourself for the hard work you put into those goals. One of the keys to motivation is seeing tangible results for your efforts. If you are working really hard and doing what you should be doing, at some point, you will tire of doing it. Especially, if you don't feel like you are making progress, or you feel like you aren't getting a reward from your efforts. It is important to learn how to create self-incentives to help drive your motivation.

FOUNDATION #7
PRACTICE LONG-TERM THINKING

Most people who are very successful have long-term goals and plans and therefore practice long-term thinking. Most successful people can very clearly articulate those plans and act with an eye toward the long term. One CEO in Japan, Masayoshi Son, not only has a five year plan and a ten year plan, but a 300-year plan! Practicing long-term thinking will keep you motivated because you will know that all your actions are in line with where you are headed! You will look at all of the decisions that you've got to make, and you will decide the answers based on the long term.

FOUNDATION #8
KEEP GROWING AND ACHIEVING

Émile Coué said, "Every day, in every way, I'm getting better and better."

In order to get motivated and stay motivated, you must keep growing and achieving. I know that sounds like an audacious statement, but it is true. The reason that most people get into motivational ruts is that they become stagnant. I have never known anyone who found stagnation to be a positive state.

At the pace that our society is changing, if you aren't growing and achieving, you aren't staying the same; you are going backward, and the rest of the world is passing you by. Growing = progress = motivation. This is one of the formulas for staying motivated.

FOUNDATION #9
PERIODICALLY EVALUATE WHERE YOU ARE

Ashleigh Brilliant stated, "Maybe I'm lucky to be going so slowly, because I may be going in the wrong direction."

If you were sailing across the Atlantic in a sailboat, you would need to constantly check to see if you were still on course. As you go through life, you need to keep checking your course in personal and professional pursuits. If you feel like you are on course, meeting or exceeding where you want to be, it can be a boost to your motivation. If you are off course, and you make some corrections, it will motivate you as well, because you have done something about it!

FOUNDATION #10
LIVE A LIFE OF BALANCE

As the old saying goes, "All work and no play make Jack (or Jill) a dull boy (or girl)."

The modern equivalent of that adage today is not only dullness, but also burnout. Working all the time, non-stop, seems to be a badge of honor for some people, but it can lead to disaster. It also can lead to a loss of motivation, where the person finally crashes and says, "Why am I doing this?"

In order to be motivated and to stay motivated, it is essential to try to live a life of balance, with a realization that sometimes it won't always be balanced. As a human being, you need to spend time on the social, spiritual, physical, and financial aspects of life, as well as the career areas.

Being in balance allows you to live a life that is richer. It keeps you in a more motivated state of mind.

In each chapter, we will be taking a look at each of these topics in more depth, and looking at each of the 10 foundations.

As you go through this book, I would encourage you to keep the following ideas in mind:

Apply it to your life

As you read this book, try to review the material and ask yourself, "How can I apply this to my own life? What does this section really mean to me?" Then give some thought on how you can apply it.

Take notes or highlight

As you read through the material, underline or note points that stand out to you, get your attention or you want to remember. Highlight it, clip it, and write in it (unless this book in your hand is from the library!) When you reach the end of each chapter, go back and review the highlighted points.

Compare

As you read through it, ask yourself how this compares with what you already know, or have already read. Then think about it and compare and contrast. Make notes accordingly.

Study

Decide this time not to just "read a book." This is about your life so *study* it. If you get distracted and miss a point, go back and reread it to make sure you "got it."

Interact

Try to think of this as more an interactive seminar rather than a book. In each chapter there will be a segment called WORKIT! And I will be asking you to work through exercises. You can skip them if you want, but remember, this is about getting motivated and staying motivated! So do the exercises, and don't skip! The choice is yours, but you will get more out of it by doing the exercises!

Discuss it

Sit down with a positive, intelligent friend or mentor. Ask to discuss the content with them, and get their feedback and advice. Be careful not to pick your favorite pessimist—they may give you feedback that can interfere with your motivation!

Challenge yourself

Challenge yourself by saying, "I am going to read this book and I am going to apply every word. I am going to do every exercise and give it 100%." Then see what happens! I am sure that your life will change as a result of your efforts.

These are the 10 foundations that are outlined in this book. I would like you to keep in mind a great quote from author Jack London as you read:

> *"I would rather be ashes than dust.*
> *I would rather my spark should burn out in a brilliant blaze than it should be stifled by dry rot.*
> *I would rather be a superb meteor, every atom of me in magnificent glow than a sleepy and permanent planet.*
> *The function of man is to live, not to exist.*
> *I shall not waste my days trying to prolong them.*
> *I shall use my time."*

I could have never said it better than that.

CHAPTER TWO

FOUNDATION #1: HAVE A PURPOSE FOR WHAT YOU DO

"Purpose is the foundation for magnificent and maximum motivation."

—Nwahs Eloyd

ONE of the most powerful sources of motivation *is to have a purpose* for what you do. At this point, you are probably saying, "OK, it doesn't take a brain surgeon to understand that I have a purpose. I get up and go to work to make money. That is my purpose."

I can understand thinking that and it seems to be a logical way to think. However, it is the wrong way to think and a thought process conditioned by society. I believe this thought process often leads to lack of motivation. Going to work to make money is not a purpose; it is a reason to go to work. Let me repeat for emphasis, it is not a purpose.

NOW AGAIN WITH PURPOSE

Let's talk about the definition of purpose. The way I define purpose is the *reason* you are on the planet (Now you understand why the "making money" definition above doesn't make sense.) Let me give you an example. Let's take two people who are both attorneys. Attorney #1 (we will call her Susan) goes to law school because she wants to make the BIG BUCKS. She graduates at the top of her class, and is a very successful lawyer. Attorney #2 (we will call her Jill) is a lawyer who decided in law school that her purpose in life was to help other people. She graduated at the top of her class, and is with a large law firm. What is the difference between Susan and Jill? Jill feels like she is doing what she was "meant to do." Susan has a restless, gnawing feeling that something isn't right and she just works too many hours, but boy the money is fabulous so...she stays. The difference is that Jill knew and defined her purpose early in her career and Susan didn't and still doesn't.

What right do I have to talk about this concept of purpose? I was a person who for the first 30 years of my life struggled to find my path.

Let's first go back to my childhood. When I was 10 years old I was lying in bed one night and I was crying. My mom came into the room and asked me what was wrong I said, "I am ten years old and I haven't achieved anything!" I seemed to somehow understand that I was meant to do something and I had the audacity at 10 years old to think I should already have begun doing something significant. (Boy, what a weird little kid!) It was about purpose.

I attended college, declared a major in theater performance because I was convinced my purpose was to entertain people and to act. The last acting class in my senior year I came to a stunning conclusion, I didn't want to act. I realized that one of my professors (who was a British Academy Award winner) couldn't make a living acting and he had to teach in order to make a living. I realized if this acting genius couldn't make a living, then I would struggle, and I wasn't willing to starve for my art. So I graduated with a B.A. in theater performance never to perform in the theater again. I exited school with my compass out searching for a direction and a purpose.

One fateful night a light shined into my window and voilà; I had a vision of what I was meant to do! (Just kidding—it didn't happen that way and it almost never happens that way except in the movies.) Searching for and finding your purpose is hard work and is a process, not an overnight decision or a sudden revelation.

I decided that I would give retail management a shot. It seems like a completely foolish idea now, but it seemed like a good idea at the time. I spent two incredibly long, horrible years in retail management, and knew that it was not the work I was meant to do. I was doing work I couldn't stand—without meaning or purpose. I would get up in the morning dreading work and go home at night dreading the next day.

I went into sales and I spent six years in sales. I was good at selling because I was a "people person." I found that I could communicate with people in a way that was convincing. I liked sales, but didn't love it. One morning the fickle finger of fate stepped in and my phone rang. It was a call from the company I worked for wanting to know if I was interested in becoming a trainer. I took the job after some research, and it changed my life in ways I am only just now beginning to understand.

I have been a training professional for some time now, and it is my life's work. I believe my purpose is to have a positive impact on other people's lives. I get up in the morning knowing why I do what I do. The pay is nice, and the people are very, very nice, but the payoff for me is knowing that I have had an impact on someone's life. Once you know your purpose, the work flows, the motivation rises, and productivity is at an all-time high.

HOW TO FIND YOUR PURPOSE

To find your purpose, follow these easy steps: 1) Find a large mountain. 2) Climb it. 3) Locate the guru in the long, flowing white robe. 4) Ask him, "Master what is my purpose?" 5) Wait for answer. 6) Leave the mountain immediately and apply!

I wish it were that easy.

There are many steps in finding your purpose. They require study, work, and some very hard soul-searching to determine what you want your life to stand for and be about. Some people are lucky and this happens to them by accident. Most people, however, have to work to find it. Here are some ideas and techniques for finding your purpose:

ONE SHEET EXERCISE

Take out a blank piece of paper. On that piece of paper write down a list of all the things you are really good at and have been good at all your life (This is not the time to be modest). You either know or have been told what you are good at all of your life.

After you have filled the page with talents or gifts, take a look at the page. Does anything stand out to you? Any common things? Let's say your list is filled with things like writing, art, brainstorming, or painting.

Maybe the central theme around the page is creativity, and your purpose is to create as your contribution to the world.

Now break your general talents and gifts into several different types of purposes, all unique. You could say: 1) I am meant to create beauty to help people relax and enjoy life more. 2) I am meant to create buildings through architecture so that people's lives are made more comfortable. 3) I am meant to create advertising that gets a message across to help people grow their business. 4) I am meant to be an inventor and to create inventions that change the world. 5) I am meant to teach other people creativity so that they can be more creative.

Get the idea? The purpose in each one of those cases is tied around creativity—but each one is very different. Try creating your list and see if anything pops to the surface.

Get real

Carve out some free time and go away to a quiet place. Take a pen and pad, and get ready to write. Take the time to ask yourself the following questions: 1) Someday, when I am old and gray, what do I want to have accomplished? Why are those things important? What contribution would they have made? 2) What are two or three things that you will regret if you do not do them in your lifetime? What do you think would stand in your way if you don't get them done? Why? 3) Why were you born? Do you think you have specific gifts or talents you were meant to use? Why? Are you using them? If not, why not? 4) Fill in the blank; I was meant to ______________. Why do you think that? 5) What is very important to you? Why? After you have gone through these series of questions, some patterns might emerge and you may be closer to uncovering your true purpose.

Ask others

Pick 10 people that you either know or have known and take an informal survey. (Okay, this one requires some real honest to goodness guts.) Ask them what they think you are "meant to do". Ask your Mom, your Grandma, or your crazy Uncle Larry. Ask your golf buddy or a co-worker.

Now you are wondering why I am asking you to do this crazy exercise. Sometimes other people can see things in you that you can't. They may give you a different view. You may say, "Wow! They are right; I never looked at it that way." I once conducted a training session in Canada. When I was done, I was packing up my materials and one man stayed in the room. He was just staring at me in a very thoughtful way. I stopped what I was doing and asked him what was up. He said, "Why are you here?" I said I had no idea what he was talking about. He told me that in his mind I should be doing training on a national scale, for a larger company, so that I wouldn't be "wasting my talent." I have to tell you, it was a real revelation for me. That person was able, at that time, to see something in me that I was not able to see.

As you get answers from people, you have to be willing to sort through and edit the answers. Be careful not to pick people who are negative or critical. This can be very valuable feedback and may lead to a revelation from the person you least expect it from.

There are no wrong answers

Keep in mind as you go through this process that there are no wrong answers. Don't let society or your own internal critic squash your life's purpose. This is your life! If the ideas that pop up seem to be absolutely absurd, relax! There is plenty of time to sort them out and think about them. Be patient and don't rush things. The answer will come in time.

Eliminate the possibilities

Take out a blank sheet of paper. At the top, write the title "All the things I hate doing". Start making a list of all the things you hate. You may put down filing your income tax, doing laundry, writing reports, or fishing in saltwater. Write down as many of these items as possible on the list. Now on the opposite side of the page (or somewhere else) write the opposite of these items. If you wrote "doing laundry," then maybe you write "shopping for clothes" and then write why you love doing that.

When the exercise is complete you will have a list of all the activities that you like and dislike, and the reasons why. Review this list and look for patterns. There may be a pattern to all the things you like and dislike that can lead to understanding your purpose.

Read the books

There is a wealth of information on the topic of developing a mission statement and finding your purpose. I recommend the following books: 1) *The Seven Habits of Highly Effective People*, Stephen Covey 2) *What Matters Most*, Stephen Covey 3) *What Color is Your Parachute*, Richard Nelson Bolles. These are only a few titles. There are many fine books out there on this topic.

The buffet plan

Try what I refer to as the buffet plan—try a little bit of everything.

- Take some community college classes in various subjects.
- Read books on topics that you have never read.
- Join a civic or fraternal organization and attend on a regular basis.
- Read a magazine that you have never read.
- Visit places that you have never visited.

The idea behind the buffet plan is to "taste" as many experiences as possible and to try and discover your true purpose.

Select a wise advisor

Find a person whose intelligence you admire and ask them to meet with you. This can be a professor, a professional, an executive, a smart friend, or a member of the clergy. Let them know that you are trying to narrow down what you are "meant" to do, or your purpose. If they are smart, they will ask you many great questions. A good coach or advisor will ask you more questions and will be reluctant to tell you what to do.

Library lookup

Go to your local library and find the non-fiction section. In the non-fiction section, just go through various areas and pick up books on topics that you have never read about before. Take the books home and review them. In your review, you may find subjects that pique your interest. Then you can decide what topics you want to investigate further.

Internet hunt

On a blank piece of paper, write down 20 topics you may have an interest in knowing more about. Once you have completed this list, go on the Internet and search these topics to see where it leads. Let the search lead you wherever it leads and see what topics grab your attention.

One evening I woke up in the middle of the night with a fever of 106°. Needless to say, I was very sick and rushed to the emergency room. I was taken quickly into the treatment area and my family doctor was called. He examined me and said I was very sick. (This I knew!) He decided I had either meningitis or encephalitis; both are very dangerous. I was told that in order to determine which condition I had, a spinal tap would need to be done. In this procedure they take a large needle and insert it in your spine in order to remove spinal fluid. It is not fun. The E.R. physician made three attempts, causing me a great deal of pain. My family doctor tried three times and failed. He probably had not done a spinal tap since medical school. By this point, I was not in a very good mood and told them in very clear language to get out of the room and leave me alone. When they tried to convince me that it had to be done, I said very loudly "FINE! Then get someone in here that knows how!!!"

A neurologist was called, and he asked the dynamic duo if I had been given anything for pain. They looked at each other and then at the floor and sheepishly said no. He gave me a sedative to relax me. He said he could do the procedure without pain. He made my soon-to-be ex-family doctor leave the room and he did the procedure. I didn't experience any pain, didn't even feel a stick. I thanked him profusely for his kindness and skill. He told me something I will never forget. He said he was a surgeon in Vietnam and had come to learn the meaning of true pain and that he felt his purpose was to provide care for his patients that was both humane and preserved their dignity as a human being. He came and saw me every day and he was smart, upbeat, and enthusiastic. This story is a classic example of the power of purpose. He wasn't just a doctor, but a doctor with a purpose.

WHY A POWERFUL PURPOSE IS IMPORTANT

I walked into my gym recently to get some advice and coaching from a personal trainer. We sat down and he said,

"OK, before we get started what is your goal?" We had a great discussion, and he said that the problem with most people he coaches as a personal trainer is that they aren't working out with a goal in mind. That was a good insight. I have given it some thought and the reason I want to work out is to: 1) Fight the ravages of the aging process. 2) Live a long healthy life free of disease. 3) Live a quality life that fitness provides. 4) Drive my energy to higher levels. 5) As a motivational speaker, I want the outside to represent the inside. This is the motivation that drives my workout and eating plan.

The reason why you do something long-term is your purpose. Your purpose is your road map to guide you through your life.

- Martin Luther King Jr. had a purpose, and that was to get America to change the way we think about civil rights.
- Mother Teresa had a purpose, and that was to provide comfort to those who were suffering.
- Zig Ziglar has a purpose, which is to motivate and inspire people in order to help them maximize their potential.
- Dr. Stephan Covey has a purpose, which is to teach people the habits of highly effective people and the importance of character.
- Thomas Edison had a purpose, to create inventions that would make a difference in people's lives.

So what is your life purpose? You may think that the people listed above are amazing achievers and that you could never reach their level. That is where you would be wrong. The people listed above were, and are, just like you and me; the only difference is that they were driven by a powerful sense of purpose.

WORK IT

This is the portion of the book when you begin to apply to your life what you just read. So let's get busy and WORKIT by answering the following questions! Let the pencil fly, and don't edit your answers, just write the first thoughts that come to mind.

IDENTIFYING YOUR PURPOSE

Make a list of things you are good at doing.

____

____

____

____

____

Make a list of 10 people you can ask the question "What do you think I was meant to do?"

1. ____________________________________
2. ____________________________________
3. ____________________________________
4. ____________________________________
5. ____________________________________
6. ____________________________________
7. ____________________________________

8. ______________________________

9. ______________________________

10. ______________________________

Make a list of all the things you hate doing.

____

____

____

____

____

Make a list of some books you could read about defining your purpose. (If you don't know, do a search on Amazon.com for books)

____

____

____

____

____

What would you like to experience more in order to learn about your purpose?

____

____

____

____

Why?

Make a list of wise people you could possibly use as advisors.

List 20 topics that you can research on the Internet.

____

____

____

____

____

____

____

____

ACTION LIST

Now that you have worked through these questions, what are three actions that you can take over the next 30 days that will bring you closer to knowing your purpose?

1. ____

____

____

2. ____

____

____

3. ____

____

____

Now write these action items on your calendar.

CHAPTER THREE

FOUNDATION #2
HAVE A PASSION FOR WHAT YOU DO

"I am a firm believer in the theory that people only do their best at things they truly enjoy."

—JACK NICKLAUS, Pro-golfer

HOW is passion defined? Webster's defines passion as: "Pervading spirit, ruling passion, master passion, fullness of heart, flow of soul."

Why is it important to feel passion for what you are doing both professionally and personally? One reason is that if you are passionate, you are motivated, and if you are motivated, you are passionate! Have you ever met someone who is passionate about his or her work? It probably made a huge impression on you.

Let me tell you about Kevin Brown. The first time I walked into the meeting room at a hotel in Philadelphia, Kevin Brown was setting up tables for my meeting. He came over with a big smile and said, "I am Kevin Brown, and I would like to welcome you to our home. I want to make sure you feel at home when you are here, and if you need anything give me a call. I am employee of the year and I will exceed your expectations, because when you care it shows." Kevin Brown works at the hotel setting up the tables for meetings and banquets. I have never had a meeting in Philadelphia at any other hotel. Kevin Brown is passionate about his work. My first question when I walk into the hotel is, "Is Kevin on duty tonight?" Kevin Brown's passion for his work is an incredible value for his employer and for him. Think about it, whenever you experience someone who is energetic and passionate in a store or a restaurant or a business, doesn't it impress you? When you experience the opposite of that, doesn't it make a negative impression?

Having a passion for what you do has several advantages:

- It keeps you fired up and motivated!
- It makes what you are doing fun.
- You can be an inspiration to others.
- You will be more productive.
- You will be more successful.

People who are passionate have more energy, enthusiasm, and charisma. It is like a high-powered jolt of electricity. A person who is passionate loves what they are doing so much that they eat, drink, and sleep it.

So you are now saying to yourself, "Yeah right, but what if I am not like that? What if I am not filled with that kind of passion? What if I never feel that kind of passion?" You may also be saying, "This guy is crazy and the passion thing is for the birds."

If I may, I would like permission to be very blunt with you (picture me up real close to your face): YOU HAVEN'T FOUND WHAT YOU ARE PASSIONATE ABOUT. If you are not passionate about your work and your life, then change it! Stop complaining and do something. Life is too short to keep doing what is passionless and mundane! But you must make that decision.

I recently stepped into an elevator and said, "Hello everyone." Everyone on the elevator looked at me like I was a little crazy and kind of mumbled. Come on! Wake up world! When you feel passionate, energized, upbeat, optimistic, and proud of what you are doing, you will be motivated and will get more accomplished than you ever thought possible.

HOW TO FIND THE PASSION

Are you married or in a committed relationship? If you are, you probably had to look around for a long time before you found the right person. How did you find the right person? More importantly, how did you know it was the right person? As your mom and dad used to say, when you are in love, "you will just know." So you knew you were passionate about this person, and they knew they were passionate about you.

Professionally, the same rules apply. You will know when you find the profession or job that you can be passionate about. In order to find out what you are passionate about, you must search anywhere and everywhere. Here are some suggestions for finding your true passion professionally and personally.

Go Back

Look back at your childhood and teen years, and ask yourself, "What was I passionate about back then?" Could it be that you still are passionate about that area? It may be an old flame that is dormant and waiting to be reignited. Take some quiet time and think through that. Can you think of something deep in the back of your mind?

Go Out

Part of the problem many of us face is that we keep doing things the same way, and doing the same activities over and over. We never do anything new. Try to read new magazines, travel to new towns, and go to a museum you have never visited. In our family, every other Saturday is "Family Day" and this sacred day is set aside to go somewhere. The family day only has one simple rule: It must be somewhere we have never been. Seeing new sights, visiting new places just may stimulate your imagination and lead you to discover a passion you were not aware existed. The bottom line is that if you haven't found you passion so far, you need to change your methods.

Vacation

If you go on vacations every year, plan to go to different places. If you live in the mountains, go to the beach. If you live at the beach, go to the mountains. The different places you go will stimulate your imagination and help you uncover your true passion for what you love. You may accidentally run into the passion of a lifetime and a new career.

Read

As Denis Kimbro, the author, says, "Leaders are readers." Read constantly and read about topics that you have an interest in knowing more about. Even if you have a slight fascination with a topic, get a book and read about it. Surf the net and try to find out more about it. Read the trade journals of that particular industry. For example, if you have an interest in being a police officer, read about police officers. Better yet, call your local police department and ask if they allow citizens to ride with them. The only way you are going to find out is to experience as closely as possible the area in which you have an interest. As the old Alka-Seltzer ad said, "Try it; you'll like it!" I recently had someone call me who was interested in the training industry. I asked them how much they knew about it. They said they knew nothing about it. I gave them several resources, said I would be happy to help them in any way I could, and to touch base and let me know how things were going. The person never called me back.

Talk to People

Every day you come in contact with many people who are involved in different professions and interests. When you meet people, take advantage of the opportunity and "pick their brain." Ask them what they do and what they like about it. Try to learn as much as possible from them to see if you can relate to it, and to see if you may have an interest in that topic.

Take Classes

Pick an area of interest and sign up for some classes at your local community college. You may find a subject that gets your wheels spinning and fascinates you! Think of this approach as a "buffet" approach; you are sampling different topics, trying to find your passion.

Audio Teaching

An additional method of discovering your passion is to listen to audio teachings. There are thousands of CDs, podcasts and audio books of seminars and classes on the market that you can listen to when you are traveling. These audios can stimulate your thinking and give you great ideas that you haven't thought of before.

Find a Mentor

Find someone who is successful and who is involved in the area that you may have an interest in learning more about. Contact them and ask them if they are willing to have lunch with you to discuss what they do and to give you advice. If they are willing to meet with you, it can be a good way to get an inside perspective on that subject.

Find a Coach

If you go to a local gym, you have the option of hiring a personal trainer or "coach" who is an expert in fitness and nutrition. Wouldn't it be nice if you could hire a "success coach?" Well there is good news. There are now personal success coaches nationwide who can coach you. For a fee, these trained professionals will work with you over the phone or in person and help with your overall life goals.

Magazines

Take advantage of magazines on the newsstand. There are tons of great business and general interest magazines as well as specialty topics. I think today there are more magazines than ever. Get magazines on topics you may be interested in and read up!

KNOWING PASSION WHEN YOU SEE IT

When you keep searching for your life passion and you finally find it, how will you know that you have found it? Here are some symptoms which are very easy to recognize:

- You will be excited about it long-term.
- Your wheels will be turning 24/7!
- Even though it is your work, you would almost be willing to do it for free.
- When time flies by, that is a big clue!
- You will give 197% willingly.
- You will talk about it with friends and family constantly.

I am sure you have heard of the comic strip *Dilbert*. This comic strip by Scott Adams is one of the most popular in the country. Scott is passionate about being a cartoonist. He wanted to be a cartoonist in the worst way and was very passionate about it. He was working at a computer company in California full-time. In order to work on his comic strip, he would get up at 5:00 A.M. every morning and work from 5:00-7:00. He would then go to work. If someone is willing to go to that extreme, he is full of passion. Do you have that kind of passion now?

HOW TO STAY PASSIONATE

Once you have done the work and you are blessed enough to truly understand where your passion lies, then you have to stay passionate. Think of it as lighting a fire. Once the fire was lit, you still would have to work on keeping it burning by adding wood every now and then. Here are a few strategies to keep your passion burning brightly:

Strategy #1

Keep your goals, thoughts, and long-term plans in front of you and in the front of your mind. Review them often to remind yourself of why you are working so hard.

Strategy #2

Have a "rough day" strategy. There will be days when everything will seem to go wrong, and it will appear that all the forces of nature are aligned against you. When you have "one of those days", you need to have a strategy on how to stay positive and to be able to maintain your motivation. For me personally, exercise is the key. A good intense workout eliminates stress. It is also probably healthier than drinking!

Strategy #3

Control your environment. There are many people who say they can't control their environment. I really have a problem with this philosophy. Why? It's very simple. People say they can't control their environment, but they have choices that they make daily. Everyone has the ability to make choices. We have the ability to pick our friends, our work, where we live. We even have the ability to pick our spouse. We also have the ability to change our environment if we aren't happy. I get tired of the victim mentality that people get caught up in and say they have "no control." The principal at my daughter's school once gave a speech about why kids at school got in trouble. The #1 reason was the kids they "hung out" with on a daily basis. He contended that parents must control who their kids "hang out" with and that each parent had the obligation to control their kid's environment.

My wife is a very upbeat and positive person. She has made a conscious decision to control her environment. If friends are negative and mean-spirited she gradually stops associating with them. If family members are at a stage in their life when they are negative, she limits contact. (After all, you can't fire your family!) She also chooses friends for the most part who are positive, upbeat, and, most of all, supportive. Find friends who will be supportive, nurturing and hold onto them for dear life!

This leads to some very difficult issues that you may have to face. In order to maintain a positive attitude, to be passionate, you must decide who in your life is supportive, and who is negative. This may mean reducing contact with some people and even not being friends with some people. I know that sounds harsh, but if someone is not supportive, but negative, and they drag you down; what good does that kind of relationship do for you or for them?

I used to work many years ago with a woman who really didn't understand the concept of controlling her environment. She was always complaining about her husband who was verbally abusive and never helped around the house. He often called her "fatty," "walrus," and other demeaning names. He was often out of a job and complained constantly. She was a hard worker who was trying to raise three kids. When we would talk, I would ask her, "Why do you put up with this?" She would say that she had no choice and couldn't change it. I would argue that every day we have choices: to accept abusive comments or not, to stay married or not, and to work where we work or not! Life is a series of choices that we make and that we can choose to keep making! Not doing anything is a choice, and we need to work on controlling our environment.

Please understand that being passionate and motivated will make you different than many people in our society. This is a great, distinctive differential, but keep in mind it will open you up to criticism. You will be the person who is saying the world is round in a world that thinks it is flat.

For some reason, people will try to negate what you are doing. They will cut you down and try to tell you all the reasons why you can't, won't, and shouldn't; and they will take pleasure in the act! Tell them politely that you really appreciate their input (kill them with kindness) and tell them you have to go because you have things to do!

I was once offered a new job, and it was a great growth opportunity. My wife and I both decided to "go for it" and I gave notice at my old job and decided to move from South Florida to Philadelphia. The negative comments were expected but still amazed me.

"You are taking a big risk."

"I can't believe you are leaving after being here eight years."

"It's a stupid mistake."

"Philly is a big city—I don't see you as being a city person."

"I don't believe you are moving to Filthy-delphia."

If we would have listened to and believed these ridiculous and incredibly negative comments, we would have never moved and we would have missed out on one of the best experiences of our lives. Don't let the negative people in this world shape your vision of the future!

You must fight the good fight and always maintain your passion for work and for life.

Have you ever met someone who is passionate about what they do? Is Phil Mickelson passionate about golf? Is Stephen Spielberg passionate about movies? Is Tony Little passionate about helping people lose weight? Is Judge Judy passionate about the law and fairness? Yes! Of course!

Having a passion will drive you on days when you need driving. It will separate you from most of the people in your society. In a job interview, passion will increase your chances of landing the job. For promotions, being passionate will increase your chances of being promoted. (If it doesn't, you may be working for the wrong company.)

Passion pushes your pure profitability potential, your productivity potential, promotion potential, and professional potential!

That is the passion differential!

WORK IT

This is the portion of the book when you begin to apply what you just read to your life. So let's get busy and WORKIT by answering the following questions! Let the pencil fly, and don't edit your answers, just write the first thoughts that come to mind.

IDENTIFYING YOUR PASSION:

What are some potential areas or subjects that you may have an interest in pursuing? Make a list.

What did you dream of being when you were a kid?

What subjects fascinate you?

Make a list of some books you could read in these potential areas (if you don't know, do a search online for books):

What are dreams have you had but have deferred or delayed?

Why?

If money was not a limitation and didn't matter, what would you do with your life?

____

____

____

____

____

Describe yourself to someone you have never met.

____

____

____

____

____

Who are some potential mentors?

____

____

____

____

____

Who has a job that you find really interesting?

____

____

____

Would they be willing to let you spend time with them on the job?

If you could take four years off and go back to school, what would you study?

In the back of your mind, what have you always secretly wanted to do that you have kept to yourself?

What talents do you have that would surprise some people?

____

____

____

____

____

____

____

ACTION LIST

Now that you have worked through these questions, what are three actions that you can take over the next 30 days that will bring you closer to knowing your passion?

1. ____

____

____

2. ____

____

____

3. ____

____

____

Now write these action items on your calendar.

CHAPTER FOUR

FOUNDATION #3
BE A NON-STOP CONTINUOUS LEARNING MACHINE

"Education costs money, but so does ignorance."

—Claus Moser

WEBSTER'S defines learning as, "To gain knowledge, comprehension, or mastery through experience or study."

I have a question that I would like you to consider. The answer has to be very honest. How many books have you read in the last month? The last three months? The last year? To show you that I practice what I preach—I can tell you that I read four books per month, twelve books a quarter and about 48 to 50 books a year. It may not seem like much, but in a twenty-year period that is over 800 books! Here is the point—some of that knowledge has to sink into my brain.

Unfortunately, many people in our society, once they have graduated from high school or college, just quit learning. They say to themselves "no more homework" and "I never have to read another book again!" They are done. Interestingly, commencement doesn't mean "finished" it means "to start." At some point these people get stagnant and eventually may lose motivation. Why? They aren't staying fresh and giving the brain of theirs the old workout.

WHAT IS A LEARNER?

What is a learner? To me a learner is someone who has an incredible thirst for knowledge. I think that learners can be identified by the following activities and characteristics:

They read books

As a continuous learner, you must read constantly. I have a rule that I have made for myself. During the year I only read books which are non-fiction, mainly "how to" books and books on motivation and success. When I am on vacation or during time off and holidays, I read fictional novels and enjoy the "mind candy" they provide. As a suggestion, you may want to set up a plan for your reading. Decide on how many books you are going to read every month and mark them in your planner. At the end of each month take out the planner and check your progress. Part of your plan should also be to decide on a reading strategy. Decide what areas you need to improve and then create a list of books that could possibly help in those areas. If you don't know of any books on that topic, go to Amazon.com and do a search, or search the computer at your local library by topic.

They ask others

Ask other people that you know and respect what books they are reading or have read that have had an impact on them. Write down their suggestions and head to your nearest local bookstore.

One of the barriers to reading a large amount of books is the fact that they are just so darned expensive. There are some creative ways around that:

Budget for it

I am sure that you budget for other items; it would be reasonable to budget for your own self improvement.

Get a library card

Most towns have a local library where books can be checked out for little or no cost. You will then have the ability to check out books by the dozen.

Watch for sales

My local "big chain" bookstore has a whole "bargain book area" where books can be bought for amazingly low prices.

Find your local used bookstore

Most communities have a local used bookstore. In my area there are two great used bookstores and I can buy 5-6 books for the price of one new hardcover. These stores have one other bonus, character that the big chain bookstores can't create.

Flea Markets and Thrift Shops

I have found many great titles for my library at flea markets and thrift shops. I have bought many classic books for ridiculously low prices.

Buying Online

There are several great websites where you can buy books. Sites like Amazon.com, BarnesandNoble.com are easy to use. They also have amazing search capabilities. You can search for books by subject, title, and author. Lastly the prices are fairly competitive and shipping is fairly quick.

We have determined that learners read, but there are other activities that learners embrace on a regular basis:

They Search the Net

You can use the internet as a source of information and research. By using many of the search engines and meta-search engines, you can locate tons of valuable information on the web. The internet is an amazing mix of websites, research, magazine articles, and commercial services that you can subscribe to for a fee. The only frustration that I have found with the internet is knowing exactly where to find the information. Because of the overwhelming amount of information, it makes sense to learn how to search the web as efficiently as possible. There are many great books on the market which teach you internet search strategies. For example, the way a topic is entered on a search engine can change the results. The topic with quotation marks around it can change the results from the search with no quotation marks. The rules are different with each search engine. Crazy, isn't it?

Ask Questions

I want you to think of A.S.K. Ask So you will Know. When a subject comes up and you don't understand something, ask! I have worked with many people in the world who will not ask a question and will pretend that they know. The only way that you can get smarter is by seeking out information which you do not understand. Seek out S.M.E.'s (subject matter experts) and tap into their expertise. My uncle, Scott Camp is the consummate "asker." He is always asking questions. We don't see each other often, but when we do, he wants to know what is going on in my life and work. When I tell him about my work and life, he then asks tons of questions. He is a human sponge who soaks up information at a rapid rate, and he is very smart. Why? Because he is a non-stop continuous learning machine. He understands that the more questions he asks, the more he will learn.

Read Periodicals and Magazines

Continuous learners subscribe to and read many different magazines every month, on many diverse topics. I highly recommend reading the magazines of your industry, magazines about business, and magazines that are about success and motivation. I also would encourage you to read magazines that relate to topics that are hobbies, or you are passionate about. You should be reading about what cutting edge companies are doing and what leading thinkers are thinking about. Reading about other people's success stories is very uplifting and motivating because when you read about people like you who have accomplished amazing things; it confirms the belief that anything is possible.

You will read it and then say to yourself, "If they can do that, why can't I?"

Watch Videos

I don't think there are many topics available that don't have videos that can help you learn about a topic or even gain new skills. For example, if you want to learn how to type or even how to type faster, there are many videos and computer programs that are on the market. These programs work well because they allow you to practice and even give you feedback. I hear people say at times, "Well, I couldn't do that. I don't know how to..." Well come on, wake up, world! If you don't know, LEARN NOW. You cannot allow the limitations of the knowledge you have now to stand in your way.

Listen to instructional audio

Every year in our country, people drive thousands of miles, literally hundreds of hours, and they listen to the radio. I have a question: How much will you learn by listening to one hundred hours of your favorite radio "shock jock"? I would say not much. I also think radio won't help you get motivated or stay motivated because radio can be the opposite: negative, mean-spirited, and depressing. The old "garbage in, garbage out" formula applies. As much as your local morning DJ is entertaining, in my opinion, you are wasting precious learning time. Decide what topics you want to learn about and find audio teachings on that topic. Some people have referred to their cars as their "rolling classrooms." There are many different types of audios. There are "how to" audios, motivational titles featuring well-known speakers, and biographies, just to name a few categories. Maximize your time by taking advantage of your driving time.

Seminars

There are many great companies that travel around the country. They conduct one, two, and three day seminars. Keep an eye out for these seminars as they are offered publicly. The seminars are generally high quality and reasonable in price.

Training Programs

Many corporations and organizations offer training programs as part of employee development. If your company offers training, sign up for as many courses as you can. In general these programs are well developed, tested and are conducted by training professionals. Take advantage of these great programs.

Employee Education Assistance

Many corporations also offer educational benefits for employees. These programs often offer reimbursement for educational courses and often will pay for a percentage up to 100%. Find out if your employer offers this benefit.

Community Schools

There are many schools in various communities that offer many non-degree classes. They have a great variety of classes in many subjects. Find out what is offered in your town and find out how to enroll. The other advantage of these kinds of programs is that they are often very inexpensive.

WHY YOU SHOULD KEEP LEARNING

The bottom line is that the world is going through rapid change and you should be willing to reinvent yourself every year. Because the world will not stay the same, you can't stay the same.

Let's take the example of Warren Sapp, a defensive lineman for the world champion Tampa Bay Buccaneers. In the 2002 season, Warren Sapp was the sharpest that he had ever been and helped take his team to the playoffs. The year before, Warren had had a bad season; he was trying to figure out why. He studied tapes in the off season and made a determination that he had gotten "fat and lazy" (his words) and apathetic. He decided that he had to get better. In the off season he dieted, worked out, lost weight, and was in the best shape of his life. If a Pro Bowl level player is willing to reinvent himself each year, shouldn't you?

Every year you have to be a better, faster, smarter version of yourself. Just like new computer software, every year you have to upgrade to a better version of you. You have to be a You 1.0, and then a You 2.0, and then a You 3.0. Be willing to upgrade!

Remember if you are not growing, you are slowing!

WORK IT

This is the portion of the book when you begin to apply to your life what you just read. So let's get busy and WORKIT by answering the following questions! Let the pencil fly, and don't edit your answers, just write the first thoughts that come to mind.

A LEARNING MACHINE

On a scale of 1-10, with 10 being the ultimate learning machine, how would you rank yourself?

1 | | | | | | | | | 10

Why did you give yourself that ranking?

What are three activities that you can start doing this week to help you start becoming a learning machine?

1.

2.

3. ____

What obstacle has stood in your way?

What books are you going to read in the next month?

In the next year?

What are some subjects that you would benefit from if you knew more about them?

____

____

____

____

____

How are you planning to learn this information?

____

____

____

____

____

How will becoming a learning machine help you in your personal and professional life?

____

____

____

____

____

____

____

ACTION LIST

Now that you have worked through these questions, what are three actions that you can take over the next 30 days that will bring you closer to being a learning machine?

1. ____

____

____

____

2. ____

____

____

____

3. ____

____

____

____

Now write these action items in your calendar.

CHAPTER FIVE

FOUNDATION #4 BE A MENTOR AND HAVE A MENTOR

"A single conversation across the table with a wise man is worth a month's study of books."

—Chinese proverb

WHAT is a mentor? *Webster's* defines a mentor as "a wise and trusted counselor or teacher."

A mentor is someone who will be your trusted advisor and coach. This is ideally a person who is smart, successful, and very perceptive. The quality of your success is in direct correlation to the quality of your mentor. Your mentor could be someone who is well known in his or her field or in the community. It could be someone who is part of your religious organization or a family friend.

GET LUCKY BY HAVING A MENTOR

I have been lucky enough to have had several mentors in my life and they have had an impact on me that is immeasurable.

Let me repeat—they have had an impact on me that you cannot possibly imagine. Why is it important to have a mentor? It is important to have a mentor for many reasons:

You can't think of everything yourself

As much as you would like to think you can, you can't think of everything! Many times when you are involved in a situation, you can't see the forest for the trees. Simply put, you may be too close to the situation. A mentor has the ability to step back from the action and to review it objectively. Let's say that you are fighting a battle on the ground, but you have a radio connection to a helicopter high above the action. That is the perspective of your mentor. Secondly they aren't emotionally involved, so they have the ability to be more objective. Lastly, it is the classic "two heads are better than one" approach. Your mentor extraordinaire may come up with ideas that are new and different. I have had mentors who have caused me to think "I wish I would have thought of that!"

You don't always have enough experience

Your mentor may have experienced the same situations in the past and have excellent advice on how to handle it. Let me give you an example. My sixteen-year-old daughter is very pretty; in fact she is model-pretty! A few years ago she came home from school one day and said, "I am ugly because no guys will ask me out." This was her perception and I was able to share with her my experience. I told her that when I was in the tenth grade and lacked confidence, that I wouldn't ask pretty girls out because I was intimidated. I know this because I experienced it. The reason guys were not asking her out is she was too pretty! So that is the advantage that a mentor can provide. There is, as they say, no replacement for experience.

Two heads are better than one

Have you ever tried to play tennis by yourself? It's pretty boring, isn't it? You don't have anyone to return your volley or to push you to the next level. Having a mentor is similar to having a great partner in tennis; it gives you someone to bounce ideas around and with help improve your game. For me, having someone to bounce ideas around has always resulted in better ideas.

Navigate the corporate culture

If your mentor is someone who works at your company, they can help you navigate the corporate culture. They can help you understand the different personalities and quirks of each person. Having this kind of guidance can be a great help and make your life easier.

Save time on your climb

A great way of saving time on your climb up the corporate ladder is to have a mentor. There are people who have already learned what you are learning and have experienced what you are now experiencing. As Brian Tracy, noted author and speaker says, "If you want to be successful, find someone who has already done it and do it the same way they did."

HOW TO SELECT A MENTOR

Success is more likely if you have a mentor, but the key is to have the right mentor. So how do you select a mentor? Here are some tips on selecting a mentor:

Find someone who is already successful at what you aspire to do

If the potential mentor is in an area that you don't aspire to, then at least make sure it is someone who is highly successful.

Don't limit yourself to just one mentor

You can have a mentor for each area of your life. You can have a mentor for your career, for fitness, finances, and for other areas you want to improve in—just make sure you don't spread yourself too thin. Too many mentors can be just as counterproductive as not having one at all.

Don't assume it has to be someone you already know personally

I met Nancy at a training event, and we were discussing mentors and mentoring. I asked her if she had a mentor and she said her mentor was a very famous motivational speaker and author. Stunned, I asked her how this happened. She said that she was at a seminar and at the end went up and asked him, and he said yes! It was as simple as that. Don't make assumptions about who would or wouldn't agree to be your mentor. Being a mentor is usually flattering, a slight boost to someone's ego. You may be surprised who will say yes.

Decide if you want your mentor to be someone from your current organization or from outside the organization

There can certainly be advantages and disadvantages with each. As mentioned earlier, someone from inside your organization can provide tremendous insight and perspective about the organization and the culture. On the other hand, people can sometimes be at a company for so long they lose perspective. Someone from outside can often provide unique perspective and insight. I once was taking a train ride back from a business trip and found myself next to a gentleman from Turkey who was very perceptive. He was asking me questions about American culture, and he also had unique perspectives about "We Americans." He was able to provide perspective that I was not able to have, but made sense once he said them. A mentor from outside can provide that kind of perspective.

Try not to pick a mentor that is too much "like you"

We are often most comfortable being around someone who is similar to us in appearance, upbringing, or beliefs. I believe a mentor is someone who will help you think outside the lines. If the person who is your mentor is too much like you, then the result will be what I call "groupthink" which is dangerous. This is when everybody in a group all start to think alike. Be different, pick someone who can give you new, fresh perspectives and challenge your thinking.

Don't limit your selection only to someone who is older

There are many bright, young minds out there that may know a lot about a specific topic. My daughter is the resident expert on VCR's, DVD's, remotes, and how all the devices work. When I am befuddled, she comes in and shows me which buttons to push. Having a younger person as a mentor means being willing to put your ego aside in order to learn. What if you had met Bill Gates when he was only 16? Could you have learned something from him?

Look to the seniors

There is, I believe, a precious asset in the nation that is wasted, overlooked, taken for granted, and grossly under-utilized. That is the remarkable population of senior citizens. This population has a remarkable wealth of experience and wisdom gained over the ages that you can tap into. They might also have more time available to spend with you and would appreciate feeling valued.

In my teens, I had a passionate interest in pursuing cartooning as a career. I had a decent amount of talent and I wanted to draw a nationally syndicated comic strip for a living. I boldly called the editor of the local big city paper. I asked for an appointment to see him, explaining that I was interested in pursuing cartooning as a career, and would love his advice. I was very surprised when he said he would see me. (Proof that it pays to ask) We had a great meeting, and he reviewed my work and was complimentary. He referred me to a local professional cartoonist, and gave me his name and number. Joe Busciglio was a cartoonist who had worked on many nationally-known comic strips. He became a great friend and mentor, and because he was in his 70's, he had a great many life lessons to share.

Most people I know don't have mentors for one reason and one reason only—they have never sought one out. Most highly successful, motivated people have had mentors throughout their life. Most people have heard of Dave Thomas of Wendy's, but many people don't know that he had a mentor in the restaurant business, Colonel Harland Sanders of KFC.

THE MENTORING PROCESS

If you want to have a mentor, then you want to make sure to get the most out of the process. As a protégé, you must have some kind of process to insure success of the relationship which is going to be formed.

First, you need to decide what your objective is for that particular mentoring relationship. It is important to ask yourself the following questions:

- Why do I need a mentor for this particular area?
- How can mentoring help me?
- What do I want to achieve short term? Long term?
- What are my strengths?
- What are my areas that need to improve?
- What specific skills can my mentor bring to the table?
- How often should we meet? When? Where?
- How will I know that I am making progress?

STRUCTURING THE MENTORING PROCESS

The process of mentoring can either be formal or very informal. I don't think it matters which, all that matters is what works for each person in the process. Secondly, it is important to be as specific as possible about what you would like to get out of the mentoring. It must be clear to both the mentor and the protégé.

A few years ago, I worked with a professional image coach. The first step she took was to complete a very thorough questionnaire. After the form was complete, we discussed the specific goals of our working together and the way the process would work. Each time we met, the sessions were very focused and specific because we knew where we were both headed.

No matter what the style of your mentor, the amount of preparation you put into it will greatly affect the success of the process. Before each meeting, write down or mentally prepare for what you would like to discuss. This makes the time you spend together more productive and meaningful.

The reason you have a mentor is to help you grow and to help you become more motivated and to stay motivated. Your efforts will affect the quality of the relationship.

A young person recently approached me in our office. They had been selected to do a presentation at a big meeting and asked if I could coach him. I became his public speaking mentor. We had an initial meeting, and I walked him through the basics of one of our public speaking training sessions. He was the consummate student, asking many questions and taking notes the entire time. He asked if I had any articles on public speaking, and when I said yes, he asked if he could make copies of them. When we finished meeting, he asked if he could meet with me in a week so that he could run some ideas by me. The next week we met, he had read all the books and articles, and had written down several questions that he wanted to ask. The process continued for several weeks. I was fortunate enough to see him give his presentation, and he did a great job. He was funny, relaxed and very well prepared. Due to his hustle and preparation, he made a positive impact on everyone in the audience. It was very important because this was his first presentation to that group. If he had not prepared—not read, studied, and practiced, and not had a mentor—he would not have done as well. Remember the quality of your efforts controls the quality of your results!

BEING A MENTOR

Being a mentor is an awesome responsibility. Recently I heard a professional athlete being interviewed on television. He said to the reporter, "Everybody says that I am a role model, that athletes are role models. Well, I am not a role model and kids shouldn't look up to me." The comment really bothered me; like it or not, all athletes are role models. Being a mentor is not only advising and helping someone by lending an ear, you are also serving as a role model. Being a role model is a serious responsibility. Being a role model/mentor is also rewarding and motivating because of the impact that you can have on someone's life. Being a mentor can come in many forms:

Situational mentor

This is mentoring someone informally by giving them advice only when they ask for it, based on a problem they are currently experiencing. In most cases, only give advice when people ask for it. There is nothing worse in most people's mind than getting "unsolicited advice". You can't be a mentor against someone's will. They must be willing to be part of the process, even if it is just for that situation. If there is not implied agreement between both parties, it is a waste of time.

Friend/mentor

It is possible to be a friend and mentor at the same time. This does not mean that friends are always mentors or that mentors are always friends. Some friends don't want advice or coaching (I can think of a few.) This is also informal and often will not be labeled as a mentor relationship. As a friend and mentor, be very careful about whom you associate with. Associating with the wrong person can be a very negative and demotivating experience. Negativity can be just as contagious as enthusiasm; it is enthusiasm's evil twin.

Social/civic mentoring

This is a great way to get involved in your community. Work with a school or an organization like Big Brothers or Big Sisters to mentor children in your area. If you want to get motivated and stay motivated, work with a child and see them learn from your life lessons, Wow!

Formal Mentoring

This is a formal arrangement, set up by your company or by yourself, and the process is formal. There is a mentor, a protégé, and both parties understand their role.

There is no question that mentoring or being mentored can be a tremendous experience and can be very motivational. When, as a result of being mentored, you grow, there is not a better feeling for you or your mentor. When you mentor someone and it has an impact, there is nothing better.

The ability to connect with another human being, to really help them, to me is a most noble calling, and the greatest honor in the world. Lastly, being a mentor, or being mentored, can have a tremendous impact on your level of motivation. Go for it!

WORK IT

This is the portion of the book when you begin to apply to your life what you just read. So lets get busy and WORKIT, by answering the following questions! Let the pencil fly, and don't edit your answers, just write the first thoughts that come to mind.

HAVING A MENTOR

For what specific topics/areas would you like to have a mentor?

Why?

Who are three people that you could ask to work with you as a mentor?

1.

2. ________________________________

3. ________________________________

What has prevented you from having a mentor in the past?

____

____

____

____

____

How do you think it would help you now?

____

____

____

____

____

____

Why?

____

____

____

____

____

____

Whom could you mentor?

How do you think this would affect you?

What are three compelling reasons why you should do this?

ACTION LIST

Now that you have worked through these questions, what are three actions that you can take over the next 30 days that will bring you closer to mentoring or being mentored?

1. ____

2. ____

3. ____

Now write these action items in your calendar.

CHAPTER SIX

FOUNDATION #5
KNOW WHAT GETS YOU STIMULATED AND MOTIVATED

"FIRE...FIRE!...When ya hot, ya hot, ya really shoot your shot ya really something!"

—*Fire!*, song as sung by the Ohio Players

IF you owned an expensive racehorse (by the way, if you do—congratulations!), you would make every effort to determine under what conditions your horse performed at its best. When it won a race, you would try to monitor what it ate and when, the pre-race preparation, the environment, the trainer. You would want to know exactly what your horse did right before the race. Then you would try to replicate those conditions to the very best of your ability in order to increase the chance of your horse succeeding.

Well, the good news is you are your own horse! You need to determine what gets you motivated and stimulated. If for some reason you are down or tired and had a rough day, the methods that you have identified will get your horse up and running again.

One day my teenage daughter and I were driving down the road and she said, "Guess my favorite movie?" After nineteen guesses, which were all completely wrong, I finally gave up. I said, "I don't know. I give up," and was ready to hear some obscure movie answer. My daughter then told me her favorite movie was *Rocky* starring Sylvester Stallone. This would be the last answer I would expect from a very pretty and feminine girl. The movie is a tough gritty story of a loser who rises from obscurity to box his way to the top. It is a movie that is dark, bloody, and violent. So I asked her why she liked that movie. Her answer? "It gets me pumped!" For my daughter, the movie isn't about boxing, it's about inspiration!

IDENTIFYING YOUR ROCKET FUEL

I have found like anyone, that there are certain books, magazines, music, and people that really motivate me. I have also found certain books, people, music, and magazines to be very draining and de-motivating. They "rain on my parade," if you will.

What are some of the motivational tools and influences that can keep you going?

Books

Have you ever read the story of someone who, despite all the obstacles that they faced, was able to succeed beyond his or her wildest dreams? Weren't you amazed and inspired? There are many books that I have read over the years that have inspired me. Biography, self-help, historical, psychology and even at times, fiction books have inspired me. You need to identify a list of books that have inspired other people and then find the ones that do the same for you. Then you will have them available when they are needed.

What is great about some books is the fact that they are timeless. The classic books, because they are based on simple truths, really don't lose their relevance. I recently read *Man's Search for Meaning* by Viktor Frankl. The book was written just after World War Two, but the principles are timeless and just as relevant today.

Once you locate books that motivate you, buy them. I know it is less expensive to get books at the library, but owning the books is a better solution because they are there for reference when you need them. Invest in yourself!

Movies/Videos/DVD's

Have you ever thought about movies that inspire you? I have several that really get me pumped. *The Elephant Man* starring John Hurt is a remarkable film about the triumph of the human spirit. I also love *Dead Poets Society*, *Tucker: A Man and His Dreams*, *Rocky,* and several others. Identify the movies you like and add them to your library.

Magazines and Trade Journals

There are several magazines and journals on the market that are about motivation or success or that you would find motivational. If your dream is to someday own a yacht, a yachting magazine might be motivational for you to read. A good magazine should, in my opinion, be entertaining, motivating, and a potential resource for ideas. I can pick up a magazine and read one article which can be well worth the price of the magazine. I once picked up *Fast Company* and read an article by Tom Peters that kept my wheels spinning for days! I was so impressed. I subscribed to the magazine and read it every month.

People

I really believe that the quality of your life is greatly affected by the kind of people that you associate with on a daily basis. You can and must pick your associations. Try to surround yourself with positive, motivated, and upbeat people. Limit your contact with people who are continually negative, pessimistic, or mean. You may say at this point, "Well, I can't pick my friends and associations." That is what you have decided to believe, but it is not the truth. The truth of the matter is that you decide every day who to make friends with and to keep that friend who has driven you crazy for years!

What about your family? You can't pick your family; they are the cards that you have been dealt in life. Most families have some jokers! However if you have members of the family that are negative and continuously difficult, limit your contact to the proverbial Thanksgiving dinner and pass the gravy.

I want you to think of negative people as "energy vampires." They just sneak up from behind and suck the positive energy and motivation right out before you even realize it!

My best friend is a gentleman named Dave. Unfortunately, we live in different states. When I call Dave, he is always positive, upbeat, and supportive. At the end of a call with Dave, I always feel better than before the call started. Friends should be the people who support and motivate you.

Will there be times when you feel less motivated? Times that you are down? Sure! The key in those times is to have a friend that you can call to help bring you back up and give you a positive perspective when you are in a "funk". Not the friend who will say, "Well, let me tell you what happened to me," and tell a sad tale of woe. If you surround yourself with positive, upbeat people, you cannot fail!

Exercise

No, this is not a misprint! I said exercise. Exercise is a superb tool to get you motivated and keep you motivated. If you want to be pumped, get in a great workout! In my mind there are two keys to exercise being a motivational activity:

1. Knowing that you have a long-term goal. (see chapter 1)
2. Finding an exercise program that you enjoy and find rewarding. If it isn't enjoyable and rewarding, it won't last long!

Here is another compelling reason to exercise. Aside from the fact that you will live a longer and healthier life, in surveys that have been done, only 16% of the people asked said they work out on a regular basis. That means that if you exercise, you will immediately separate yourself from 84% of people that you may be competing against. That is a competitive edge!

Exercise, as you have probably heard many times, releases many chemicals such as endorphins, which are "natural highs". I find that exercise gives me more energy and more confidence. Try it; you will like it. If you don't like it, try some other form of exercise until you find one that you really like.

Music

Imagine the great movies of our age without music. Can you imagine *Jaws* without music? *Gone With the Wind*? *Star Wars*? This proves that music can have a powerful impact on people, and it can have a powerful effect on you! Whenever you are feeling "down" or feeling less than motivated, use music as a tool to help you get back up. Find out what kind of music gets you going. It may be music from a soundtrack, from a movie, or a play. It may be a specific kind of music like rock, country, or rap. Here is the key guideline; it has to work for you.

Role Models

It is a useful technique to identify people from the past and present that you admire that you can use for role models. Reading and studying about other people who have been highly successful can help you become more motivated. I am a big fan of Walt Disney, and whenever I read about him and all that he achieved, I just get completely fired up. When I read about all of the adversity he overcame and that he succeeded in spite of everyone's predictions, it makes me want to work even harder at achieving my goals.

Theatrical Shows

I think one of the reasons why Broadway shows are so popular is that great musicals have always been inspiring.

Maybe it is because I am of Irish descent, but whenever I see the show *Riverdance* my heart soars! Find what kind of shows get you going, whether it is musicals, dramas, or operas.

THE POWER OF OTHER ENVIRONMENTS

Find out what other kinds of environment get you going and get your wheels spinning. To get motivated, maybe visit to your local museum, visit to a certain store, or take a trip to your favorite coffee shop. Perhaps a nice walk in your favorite park, or a visit to the local luxury car dealer to look at the car you are going to own!

The bottom line in this chapter is to really understand yourself well enough to know what the keys are to your motivational lock. It is important to know the activities that get you motivated, keep you motivated, and help you to be in an "up" mood instead of a "down" mood.

Don't get me wrong, everybody gets down on occasion and that is okay. What isn't okay is to stay there! I don't think someone in a foul mood has ever accomplished anything productive. One proven method to get out of a down mood or frame of mind is to do something. Call a friend, go for a walk; just do something!

If you work at identifying the activities that really help bring you up, then (like a doctor) write your own prescription to solve the problem.

One thing I can guarantee, it is almost impossible to stay down when you are doing one of your "mood lifter" activities. There are so many people who seem helpless, trapped in dull boring lives. They are "in a rut". I think it is tragic, if they only understood they are the ones who control the quality of the life they live.... Don't live "a life of quiet desperation!" Decide that you are going to lead an exciting, productive life of motivation!

WORK IT

This is the portion of the book when you begin to apply to your life what you just read. So let's get busy and Workit by answering the following questions! Let the pencil fly, and don't edit your answers, just write the first thoughts that come to mind.

KNOWING WHAT GETS YOU MOTIVATED

What specific tools can you list that can help you stay motivated?

Why do you think these work for you?

What are the specific circumstances that tend to lower your motivation?

What are some techniques you could use to stay motivated that you haven't used so far?

How do you think they would help?

What are three compelling reasons why you should do this?

ACTION LIST

Now that you have worked through these questions, what are three actions that you can take over the next 30 days that will bring you closer to staying motivated on a more consistent basis?

1. ______________________________

____

____

2. ______________________________

____

____

3. ______________________________

____

____

Now write these action items in your calendar.

CHAPTER SEVEN

FOUNDATION # 6
REWARD YOURSELF FOR ACHIEVING

"Happiness is its own reward."

—ANONYMOUS

WEBSTER'S defines reward as, "something given or received in recompense for worthy behavior." I think that is a pretty solid definition. I would define reward as giving yourself a dividend for all the hard work you have invested so that you have a validation that your hard work is paying off. This helps increase motivation so you will continue wanting to work.

Let me give you an example. My father, Jack, is a successful man and has always been a person with an incredible work ethic. He grew up poor in a small town in the South and through grit and hard work, he literally pulled himself up from manual laborer, to factory worker, to highly paid sales executive. When he reached a certain point in his career, he went out and bought a brand new Cadillac. I was a kid at the time and I didn't understand why he had bought, in my view at the time, "an expensive, gas guzzling" car. I asked him one day when we were driving, "Dad, why did you buy this car?" He smiled at me as we were driving down the road. He told me that when he was a kid, he always saw successful people driving big cars and made a vow to himself, that if he ever "made it" he would reward himself by getting a Cadillac. It had always been a dream of his and now it had happened. He smiled a lot that year.

The story illustrates a key point. It is very important to reward yourself for achieving your goals. It is important to reward yourself for the following reasons:

- You will feel like you are making progress.
- To have a tangible reminder of why you are working so hard.
- To finalize the achievement of a specific goal.
- To help measure your progress and celebrate it.
- Because it feels great and motivates you even further.

SUCCESS IS A BLOW DRYER

I once read an interesting story about the author Steven King and his wife Tabitha. He and his wife struggled for years as he tried to make a living as a writer. They didn't, as the saying goes, have "two coins to rub together". He finally made it and signed a very lucrative book deal. He told his wife that they had finally "made it" and she asked "does that mean I can afford to buy a blow dryer now?" She had not been able to afford a blow dryer and now a blow dryer was in reach. She said that blow dryer, when she bought it, meant a great deal to her, more than anyone can imagine.

As we have discussed in other chapters, it is essential to have goals, both short and long term. It is also vitally important to tie to those goals, specific rewards.

Let's say for example that you want to lose weight. You are making a commitment to a diet and exercise program. The first step would be to decide on the specific goals long-term. Let's say your goal was to lose 50 pounds. That would be the long-term goal. Next, you would need to break it down into specific short-term goals. Let's say, you decide that it is reasonable to lose 2 pounds a week. It is great to have the long and short term goal and to have the specific details in writing, but this is where most people stop. A missing part of the equation is the setting of long-term and short-term rewards. It may be a trip, a special piece of clothing, or a new type of fitness machine that you have spotted in the stores (this is great choice because it is a reward, but tied specifically to the goal you are trying to reach). The long-term goal and the long-term reward have now been set.

Next, it is time to establish a short-term reward which is tied to the benchmarks that you have set along the way. For example, the first short-term goal may be "to lose 10 pounds." Maybe it is a trip to your favorite salon for a manicure, or the purchase of a small item. When you use this "carrot and stick" reward system, you will be so fired up that nothing can stand in your way!

Every time I have been promoted, my family has taken me out to dinner to celebrate. Why? My wife and my daughter inherently understand the value of reward. I think that deep inside, we all understand the value of reward because we all grew up in school systems that rewarded performance. We saw people get rewards for honor roll, athletic achievement, and awards for other activities. I think that as adults, we forget that reward is important. Or we know it is important and just get too busy to reward ourselves.

I have had my eye on a very sophisticated and expensive fitness machine for a long time. I watched the commercials; I ordered the video and reviewed the literature. I just had a hard time with the decision because of the expense. I received a significant promotion at work, my wife ordered it for me as a reward, and I was quite shocked when it arrived. I was grinning from ear to ear. When I see that machine, I don't see the machine: I see a symbol of my achievement! It is absolutely essential that you can see tangible results of your hard work.

There are people I know that are really into yard work. When I ask my buddy, Bob, about it, he says he likes yard work because he is outside, it is good exercise, and he enjoys it. Here is a theory: I think the reason that most people enjoy yard work is simply this, when they are done, they can see a tangible, visual result of their effort. In life, most goals attained don't have as obvious or visible results that we can stand back and look at and say, "I did this!" That's why it is so very important to reward the achievement of your goals.

A MIND IS A TERRIBLE THING NOT TO REWARD

Let me make a very important point here. This is not about rampant materialism or greed or selfishness. This is about psychological reward. As much as we would like to think we can't be manipulated, we can be influenced easily. Human beings are taught to crave appreciation and reward by the way we were brought up. It is just the way we are wired. If the idea of material possessions as a reward bothers you, then you can decide on other kinds of rewards, such as spending a weekend camping, or a visit to your favorite museum, or a visit with a friend who lives in another state. Because it is your reward system, it is entirely up to you to decide on the reward.

I believe that the reason people give up hope, lose their zest and motivation, is the lack of reward. They get up every day, go to work, work really hard, and at the end of the week, they get a modest check. By the time they pay their bills there is nothing left. It's the classic rendition of the Tennessee Ernie Ford song: "I owe my soul to the company store." There is an endless cycle of work hard, pay bills, work hard, pay bills. This creates an endless cycle with no reward. This creates a sense of hopelessness. Ironically, the very person that is caught up in the cycle creates this situation. The cycle is created by not having specific goals and reward mechanisms.

Now a word of warning: Many people will set goals both short and long term with a reward mechanism. They truly make a commitment to the process, and they reach the goals that they set. At that point, they stop short and back off of the reward that they had planned. They may say, "Well, this is kind of expensive" or "I will wait until later." This is a huge error! By setting the goals and agreeing on a reward for achieving it, you have programmed your subconscious. When you back off from the reward portion, you are setting yourself up for failure the next time. Your brain will say, "We are setting a goal and a reward," another part of you will be saying "Yeah right, last time there was supposed to be a reward and it didn't happen!" So in the simplest of terms, your subconscious mind will feel cheated, and so will you.

I am very fortunate. As a child my parents were always reinforcing the work hard/set goals/get rewards model. One summer at the age of ten, I worked really hard babysitting, mowing lawns, and saving every penny for the apple of my eye, a drum set! When I was 2/3 of the way to my goal, I was surprised by my parents who gave me the last 1/3 of the money to buy the drum set. Of course they enhanced the message by buying the drum set and having it sitting in the living room when I came home from school. I will never forget what they said. "We are very proud of you and the hard work you have done this summer. We have been impressed that you saved every penny. This is the reward for all the hard work." That reinforced the message for me in a very powerful way.

I also would suggest that as a parent, friend, manager, or colleague that you use the mechanism of reward. The technique can work with other people and can help motivate and inspire them. As a manager, I have often taken team members to lunch as a reward to thank them for their hard work. I also have found notes, letters, or memos to be a very effective motivational tool. As a parent, it is essential to teach your children the value of setting goals, achieving them and being rewarded. This is a concept that they can carry with them to a successful future and life.

There was an ad campaign in the past for Toyota, which was "Oh what a feeling!" If you practice the technique of setting goals and rewarding yourself, you will be using a motivational tool which is the fuel that will drive your passion and motivation. With goals and rewards you will truly be unstoppable!

WORK IT

This is the portion of the book when you begin to apply to your life what you just read. So let's get busy and WORKIT by answering the following questions! Let the pencil fly, and don't edit your answers, just write the first thoughts that come to mind.

REWARD YOURSELF FOR ACHIEVING

What specific rewards can you think of for rewarding your short-term goals?

What specific rewards can you think of for rewarding your long-term goals?

What are the specific circumstances that tend to make you hesitate on rewarding yourself?

____

____

____

____

____

What are some rewards that are different you could use to stay motivated that you haven't used so far?

____

____

____

____

____

How do you think they would help?

____

____

____

____

____

____

What are three compelling reasons why you should do this?

1. ______________________________________

____

____

2. ____

____

____

3. ____

____

____

ACTION LIST

Now that you have worked through these questions, what are three actions that you can take over the next 30 days that will bring you closer to staying motivated by designing rewards for your accomplishments on a more consistent basis?

1. ____

____

____

2. ____

____

____

3. ____

____

____

Now write these action items on your calendar.

CHAPTER EIGHT

FOUNDATION #7
PRACTICE LONG-TERM THINKING

"The best way to predict the future is to invent it."

—Alan Kay

ONE of the key characteristics of highly successful and motivated people is that they practice the fine art of long-term thinking. Donald Trump always has had a five-year plan. Many successful athletes and businesspeople have commented in interviews about their long-term plans. Many famous football coaches have five-year plans that they discuss with the press when they are hired. Of course, most of them are on five-year contracts!

I recently read of an Asian businessman who is a multi-millionaire. He was being interviewed by a reporter about the plans for his company. The reporter was amazed that the man had a five-year and a twenty-year plan for his company. The reporter thanked him for the interview and as he was leaving, the business man said, "Yes, but you haven't asked me about my '100-year plan.'" The businessman had a 100- and a 300-year plan laid out for his company. And we wonder why he is so successful?

GO LONG

One of the essential ingredients for success and for staying motivated is to have a long-term plan. This will allow you to think long-term instead of short-term. Think of your life going forward as a giant chessboard. If you were able to stand above the board with a five-year view, would it affect the moves you made? Of course! Long-term thinking is the act of moving many moves ahead. This has an impact on your decisions because they get easier with an eye toward the results in the future not just the present.

Let me give you an example. My wife and I many years ago wanted a house, but we couldn't afford a down payment on a standard house. Using long-term thinking, we found a deal on a small modest townhouse. We made an offer, and the offer was accepted. We didn't want a townhouse at all, but we knew the townhouse was the road to a free-standing home later down the road. A few years went by, and we sold it and moved into a "regular" house. Using long-term thinking we were able to use the "trade up" theory to finally reach the destination we wanted in the first place. The first house was not the house we always wanted, but it was a good step in the right direction. Finally we bought the home we live in today and we could live here the rest of our lives and be happy. The journey from townhouse to the house we really wanted was done in three moves: Townhouse, House #1, House #2.

If you had to get up very early every day in order to get the work done, and you had to work late every night in order to finish your work, after a while you would lose your motivation and it would start to fade. However if you know with absolute certainty that in only five years you would be paid one million dollars, you would be willing to do the hard work with that long-term thought in mind. You would cheerfully and enthusiastically do the work. That is the magic and motivation of long-term thinking. It is the fuel that keeps you going when others stop.

Let's take a look at Arnold. You know the Arnold that I mean—the muscle-bound bodybuilding champion, actor, producer, director of dramatic and comedic films, and politician He practices long-term thinking and always has. When he was growing up in Austria, he often told his friends, "I am going to America to become Mr. Universe, and then I am going to be a big movie star in Hollywood." His friends all laughed at him of course, but Arnold practiced long-term thinking, so he just smiled because he had a master plan. He moved to America, became a five-time Mr. Universe, and a star was born on the silver screen in Hollywood.

This was all accomplished despite hardships and great odds. He had to battle against the handicap of a heavy accent. Next he was told he was good in action films but couldn't do comedy. Of course he defied all the odds and succeeded beyond all expectations, all because he practiced long-term thinking. Here are some tips on getting started with long-term thinking:

Take a step back

Pick a quiet part of the day when you can really think without being rushed. Think about your life up to this point. Where have you been? What have you done? What was it that got you there? If you were to draw a map of your life up to this point, what would it look like? Now, look forward and ask yourself the same questions with a forward perspective. Where are you going? What do you want to do? After you answer these questions, use them to formulate a plan and start today.

Start practicing daily long-term thinking

When decisions come up on a daily basis, ask yourself the following question, "Does this tie into my long-term plan?" Let's say you get a call from an old friend who is starting a brand new business venture. He is looking for investors and needs about $20,000. The business is a great concept, and if it succeeds you can triple your money in one year. If it fails you can lose all your $20,000. The question must then be asked, does this tie into your long-term plan? Does the money being made tie into your plan? If the money is lost does it affect other long-term plans that you have made? It may relate to a long-term financial plan, a long-term entrepreneurial plan or some other plan that you have. This makes the decision a little easier.

Look at your life in bigger "chunks"

We have a tendency to calendar our days very tightly, and that is a sign of excellent planning and preparation. However, the problem with looking at a calendar is that we are looking at next week, next month, but rarely at next year or the next three years. If the opportunity presents itself in conversation, I often ask people about their "five-year plan." When I ask that, most people look at me like I am balancing 50 plates on my head. Most people don't have any idea, and 9 out of 10 have never thought about the next five years. I believe that one of the keys to motivation is having the courage to ask the right questions and sometimes, difficult ones. The quality of the answer is only as good as the question.

Just because you have a long-term plan doesn't mean you can't change it

At one time in my life I decided I wanted to be an actor. I saw a play and I was truly inspired and decided to change my major to drama. I was in an acting class my senior year and I experienced what I will call a "Lightning Moment." This is when the obvious strikes you like a powerful thunderbolt and you "get it." I realized I was sitting in class being taught by a brilliant man who was a British Academy Award winner. It occurred to me at that very moment that if he couldn't make a living acting then I knew I couldn't make it as an actor, and more importantly, I didn't want to pursue it. That realization struck me like a huge universal truth and I changed my long-term plan then and there. It is okay to change your plan because after all, it is *your* plan!

This is messy

Practicing long-term thinking and having a plan is messy. It is a process. You will stumble and start over. You may change your mind several times. But remember that in order to get motivated and stay motivated you have to be working from a long-term mindset. Do you remember the hidden pictures that became popular several years ago? The picture where you stare at it a long time, and eventually a picture "reveals itself?" Long-term thinking is like that. If you keep at it, a picture will emerge.

Be patient

Don't get frustrated. The essence of long-term thinking is that it is LONG TERM. It is not a sprint, it is a marathon. I get frustrated because today as a society, we are in the instant gratification mode and everybody wants everything *now*. The reality is that most things that are worthwhile take time. The stars that we all see that are "overnight sensations" have worked for years before they hit the "big time." As the old saying goes "Rome was not built in a day." This also applies to a life and a career.

Visualize

Practice long-term thinking by constantly visualizing where you are going. If part of your long-term thinking is to own a huge mansion, visualize that big mansion. Where will it be? What will the architecture look like? How big is it? What color will it be? How about the carpet? How about the ceilings? The deck? The pool? You need to visualize that mansion over and over. Better yet, find a picture of the mansion of your dreams, cut it out, and display it where you can see it. Find a mansion in your town that resembles the dream home you want, then drive by and see it every now and then. (Just don't go by too often, you may make them think you are a stalker!)

Change your language

When you talk out loud or talk to yourself (I know you do), make sure you are talking in a way that keeps you motivated.

Instead of saying, "If I become a manager," say, "When I become a manager." Remember that your subconscious is listening to everything you say and everything you do. Create a positive self-expectation that leaves no room for doubt. Just be careful about how you use this technique. Some of the negative people in the world would love to misinterpret what you are saying as "cocky" or as egotistical. Ignore those people behind that curtain! They dare to question the great and powerful you?

Set benchmarks

In order to stay motivated, it is important to set benchmarks along the way. If, for example, you wanted lose fifty pounds, you would be much more motivated if you set benchmarks along the way. It may be benchmarks relating to number of weeks working out, weight loss at the end of one month, number of days on the diet. These benchmarks will let you track your performance along the way; if you walk in baby steps, you can be more motivated as you achieve each step. Another idea is to write down the steps to your goal. Let's say there are 15 steps to reaching the goal. After you have achieved each step, you can check it off the list.

So now you can see the utmost importance of long-term thinking. It is valuable and important for a very compelling reason. The reason is that practicing long-term thinking is really the way to make your life count. As most of us realize, we only have one lifetime. The idea is to squeeze this life for all it is worth. Ideally when you are older and appreciating the golden years of retirement, you want to look back on your life and say, "Wow...what a life I had, and I did some great things."

To me the biggest tragedy of all is not when someone dies early. The biggest tragedy of all is when someone dies of old age having squandered their maximum potential.

WORK IT

This is the portion of the book when you begin to apply to your life what you just read. So let's get busy and WORKIT by answering the following questions! Let the pencil fly, and don't edit your answers, just write the first thoughts that come to mind.

LONG TERM THINKING

What specific rewards can you think of for practicing long-term thinking?

____

____

____

____

____

What has stopped you from practicing long-term thinking in the past?

____

____

____

____

____

What would you like to do long term?

____

What would you need to do to make it happen?

How do you think this would impact your life professionally?

What do you need to change about your language when discussing the future?

ACTION LIST

Now that you have worked through these questions, what are three actions that you can take over the next 30 days that will bring you closer to staying motivated on a more consistent basis?

1. ____

____

____

2. ____

____

____

3. ____

____

____

Now write these action items on your calendar.

CHAPTER NINE

FOUNDATION # 8
KEEP GROWING AND ACHIEVING

"Stagnation is the death of excellence."

—SHAWN DOYLE

HAVE you or a friend ever been in a rut? You probably have known someone who was in a rut, living a life of routine, monotony, and dullness, maybe even depressed.

Do you have a friend or know someone who is excited? Upbeat? Energetic? What is the difference between the two?

I believe the difference between the first person and the second is that the first person is not growing and achieving.

The human mechanism, I believe, is wired naturally for growth and development. As children, we are growth machines physically, emotionally, and mentally. We go to school, take dance lessons, play in sports leagues, and join the scouts. These are all activities that lead to growth and achievement. Then, after all those years, we graduate and get a job. That's when some of us put on the brakes and just stop learning and growing. We are "busy" with work, family, bills, and chores. The idea and practice of growth and achievement goes away for some of us as life takes over. Then at some point, the drive and motivation slips away, and we are in the rut. We get stagnant.

Have you ever seen a swimming pool at the end of the winter? It is dirty and overgrown with algae and mold, and it looks like it can never be restored. It has been stagnant for three seasons. It hasn't been cared for, and there has been no activity. I believe that we as humans operate in a similar fashion. If we are not active and engaged, we stagnate.

Many studies with the elderly have tried to uncover some of the reasons for senility and the slowing of mental abilities. Shockingly, they found the reason to be the lack of activity and lack of stimulation; in other words, they had grown stagnant! This is proof that when the brain isn't used, the capacity lessens.

So one of the questions that you should ask yourself is, to loosely quote Janet Jackson, "What have you done for you lately?" In other words, what have you learned in the last year? Not by accident, or because it was part of your job, but what have you learned on purpose? What have you gotten better at? How have you grown?

GROWTH IS REQUIRED AND EXPECTED

Why must you keep growing and achieving? Well, we live in a fast, crazy, and rapidly changing world, and change is happening at a more rapid pace every year. If you stay the same and don't grow, you are actually going backwards while the world passes you by! In order to stay competitive and to keep up with change, you have to grow and get better every year. This will also keep you motivated because you will have a feeling of accomplishment each year.

In a recent book, Deepak Chopra said that the human body is in a constant state of change biologically. We have new skin every 5 days, and a new liver every eight weeks. So the person we see in the mirror is in a state of constant change, and there is a new "we" every few weeks. If that is the case, shouldn't we be willing to keep growing intellectually, spiritually, professionally, and personally?

I recently went back to the town that I had grown up in, Martinsville, Virginia. I can't even begin to tell you how shocked I was! The house I had grown up in had been bulldozed; it was now an empty lot. Roads were gone, stores were closed and torn down, new shopping centers had been built, and institutions that were the lifeblood of the town were vapor. The reality is that the world is changing around us daily but we just don't notice. When we go back to a town after a long absence, the changes are much more apparent. If the world around us is changing, should we not change with it? Be willing to reinvent yourself!

Here are some tips to help insure that you keep growing and achieving:

Set Goals

Once a year, sit down in a quiet spot and really look at your goals for the year. Analyze what you did last year and all the accomplishments. You may be surprised by what you have been able to do. Next, set goals for yourself for the next year. Look at each important area of your life. Next, look forward 3-5 years and ask, "What do I want to be doing in five years?" See if the goals for the upcoming years are helping you to head in that direction.

Learn

Set a goal of reading a certain number of books for this year. Mainly read non-fiction on areas which you need to improve. Take a class. Go to a seminar. Learn a new skill. Everything that you learn is linked to everything you know and do. Therefore, learning will enhance every aspect of your life.

Experience

Arrange to experience new things that you have never done before. If you have never seen a symphony, go see one. If you have never seen a certain town, go visit it. If you have never played paint ball, do it! The more new things you experience the more you grow. Try new directions, and your life will be enhanced.

Aim for your weaknesses

Create an all-out assault plan for attacking your weaknesses. Target them and work on making them less of a liability. Do you remember the old TV show *Kung Fu*? There was a famous scene in which "Grasshopper" went to the master for advice. The master replied, "Remember, Grasshopper, it is a strength to know your weaknesses." Analyze your weaknesses and then pick two or three that you really want to attack. Develop an action plan to start working on them. Don't wait to work on them, start working on them tomorrow! As soon as you start moving forward, you will be motivated, because you will feel that you are making progress. I am a very creative person and very right-brained. This makes me tend to be unorganized. Because I have identified this as an area of weakness, I have been able to make significant progress in this area.

Decide what you don't know

Be observant and notice throughout the year what information you don't know. This is information and knowledge that either you want to have or need to have. Let's say you are an accountant and there are some new accounting procedures you keep hearing about. Ignorance, contrary to the old saying, is not bliss; find out! Attend an industry conference, call someone in the industry, buy a book, go on the internet, and dig! Find out and be curious. You will grow professionally and personally and your credibility and confidence will be increased, as will your motivation.

Exercise

There is no question that if you want to keep growing and achieving; you need to exercise. I am not saying you have to look like a world champion bodybuilder or run like a track star. I am saying that exercise will help you grow and improve your physical and mental health. Your exercise should be regular and consistent, and should include both anaerobic and aerobic exercise. Lastly, exercise will give you energy and vitality, and you will feel GOOD about yourself.

Network

They say that "birds of a feather flock together." Decide what birds you are going to flock with. Network with people who are dynamic, goal-oriented, and growing. Find out about and try to meet the people in your industry who are "in the know" and network with them.

So you, your body, and your mind are wired to grow and achieve. To not grow and achieve is not what you are meant to do. Lastly, if you are growing and achieving, not only will you be motivated, but you will also be a source of inspiration and motivation for others.

WORK IT

This is the portion of the book when you begin to apply to your life what you just read. So let's get busy and WORKIT by answering the following questions! Let the pencil fly, and don't edit your answers, just write the first thoughts that come to mind.

KEEP GROWING AND ACHIEVING

What are some specific goals you want to work on this year?

Why do you think these would work for you?

What are some obstacles you may have in achieving these goals? What can you do to get around the obstacles?

____

____

____

____

What do you need to learn?

____

____

____

____

____

____

What are some new experiences you would like to try?

____

____

____

____

____

What are three weaknesses that you can target for improvement?

1. ______________________________________

____

2. ______________________________________

____

3. ____

____

What don't you know that you should?

____

____

____

____

____

ACTION LIST

Now that you have worked through these questions, what are three actions that you can take over the next 30 days that will bring you closer to staying motivated on a more consistent basis?

1. ____

____

____

2. ____

____

____

3. ____

____

____

Now write these action items in your calendar.

CHAPTER TEN

FOUNDATION #9 PERIODICALLY EVALUATE WHERE YOU ARE

"The unexamined life is not worth living."

—SOCRATES

IF you were blindfolded and taken to a foreign country where you had never been and dropped off in the middle of a city, you would at first have trouble finding your way around. You would ask for directions, and then you would probably buy a map. Once you had the map and you knew the exact direction you were headed, you would find your way home. Because you are an intelligent person, you would stop along the way periodically and check with a local to see if you were going in the right direction. This would give you the confidence and assurance that you were headed in the right direction.

THE MOTIVATIONAL MAP

I would suggest that goals are part of your map to success. An additional part of success and motivation is stopping to evaluate your progress and to periodically evaluate where you are. This will tell you if you are on track.

Let me give you another example. Let's say you were on a workout and fitness program. If you were on that program, you would measure your body fat, weigh yourself, and possibly take measurements of your waist. This is how you would measure your progress. It would keep you motivated because as you lost weight and inches, you would be even more fired up because you had seen results!

In order to get motivated and stay motivated, it is absolutely essential to evaluate where you are on a monthly or quarterly basis for all of your goals. Doing this will have several advantages:

- It allows you to objectively stand back and take a time out in order to evaluate where you are and how you are progressing compared to the goals you have set.
- If you are meeting your goals or exceeding them, you will be that much more motivated. It feels good to be on track or ahead of schedule.
- If you are off the mark, this will give you a chance to make adjustments. This is good news because you would rather correct your course earlier rather than later. This is much better than waiting until the end of the year to fix it.
- The exercise of periodically looking at where you are will reinforce why you set out to approach the goals that you have in the first place.

The act of looking at your progress and where you are is very valuable and relevant. As members of the human race, we are always changing, and sometimes as we change, our goals and our direction changes as well. In looking back at the goals, you may decide that you want to change some of the goals you have set, and that is healthy.

ASK AND YOU SHALL RECEIVE

In reviewing your progress, ask yourself some very in-depth questions and think through the answers. As a young man, I thought that I wanted to be an actor. As mentioned in an earlier chapter, I realized I didn't want to live in New York or L.A. I realized I didn't want to be an actor and sacrifice as much as it was going to take. This was the result of asking myself the question, "Is this what I really want?" The answer in my head was, of course, a resounding no.

As you take this journey called life, it is very easy to get in a big hurry and to not stop and think about what you are doing and why. Asking yourself the right questions and really thinking about the answers will lead you to your own truth. The truth will be the key to staying motivated because what you are going after is your own.

TO BE OR NOT TO BE

Here are questions that you need to consider. Take some quiet time and find a spot where you won't be distracted and ask yourself some of these questions:

What were the original goals, and why did I set them?

Take a look at the original goals and ask yourself why you set them. What are you going to get out of these goals? Why are they important to you? How would achieving them affect your life and those around you? If you can nail down the answers to these questions it can be a fire-starter for your motivation. You may say, "That's right, now I remember why this is so important."

How am I doing against my goals that I set?

Take a look at this area and determine if you are ahead of schedule. If you are ahead of schedule, you will be very excited! You may find that you are right on track. That should be pleasing as well because you can see that you are right where you should be. You may be behind schedule; in that case, you need to decide what obstacles are standing in your way and take some action! At one point during the writing of this book, I got bogged down with being busy in other parts of my life, and at times the progress was slow. I went back a few times and made adjustments in order to get things moving again. An Asian philosopher once said, "the secret of life is the constant readjustment to our surroundings." So this constant process of evaluation and adjustment is necessary and motivating. It is also important to get a handle on how you are feeling about your progress so you can manage your feelings. If you are frustrated or upset, you need to take action to get out of that mode because it is not a mode that is productive.

What can I do differently?

Ask yourself if you are taking the right approach. What have you learned in the last three or four months that you can apply? What modifications can you make to your habits? To your lifestyle? When can you make the changes? Where can you make them? How can you make them? Is there anyone who can help you or give you advice? This is a key point. Many people are shy and reluctant to ask other people for help. I think they are concerned the other person will say no or will feel "put out" or taken advantage of. I have found in my experience that most people are flattered when you ask for their advice or help because it appeals to their ego. I also think people in general are nice and want to help. I have had very few people turn me down cold when I have asked for help, and in general, people have been much more helpful then I expected. The power is just in the act of asking for help. Try this technique; it really works.

How do you feel about where you are today?

Are you very excited about your progress? Are you not excited at all? If you aren't, why not? What is holding you back from making the progress that you want to make? What are the barriers standing in your way? Going back to the trip analogy, if you were taking a long trip across the Atlantic, would you be frustrated if after 50 days you had made little progress? Of course you would! But that would be the time you would want to adjust your course! Then you would at least feel better by knowing you were off course and have made the necessary corrections.

What is your primary objective for this goal?

Why did you set it to begin with? Why is it so important? What impact will this have on your life? It is very important to ask yourself these questions because they can be helpful reminders as to why you started in the first place. One of the primary factors in motivation, I believe, is the "why" motivation. You have to know why you are doing something; otherwise, you will at some point stop wanting to do it.

What has changed since I last evaluated?

Have there been any changes? What has changed with you? What has changed in your company? Your family? Your community? Your world? Because decisions aren't made in a vacuum, it is important to look at all the factors that could, did, or will affect your decisions. If any changes have occurred, you may need to modify your course of action.

How does this particular goal relate to the other goals I have set?

Is there an interrelation between the goals? Are any of the goals in conflict with one another? Let's say you have a goal of spending more time with your family. A second goal is to work out six times a week and really get in shape. A third goal is to go back to school and get your master's. As you can see, if you try to achieve all these goals at once, there might be an inherent conflict.

Are you having fun?

If you aren't having fun, the questions that you answered on the last few pages don't matter. If you are not having fun, at some point you will run out of steam and stop working on your goals. So I think that one benchmark should be that you are having fun! I was at an amusement park recently and watched a sixty-year-old man get on a ride. As he was buckled in, I had him in perfect view. I wanted to see how he would react. He was smiling and yelling and saying, "Whoa! This is great!" and he was having a ball! I mention this because there were other people at the park that day who were the same age and looked like they were having no fun at all! Why? They had the "I am too old to ride this ride and I will look like a fool" mindset. What a shame.

What are you doing well?

As you go through this process, write down what you are doing well. It is important to recognize and acknowledge what is going well for two reasons: first, so you can keep doing it and second, so you have a sense of accomplishment. Even if some things are not going well, other aspects are going well.

Where are the key areas for improvement?

If you had to identify one or two areas off the top of your head that could use improvement, what would they be? What kind of impact would improving these areas have?

What would make a huge difference?

If you think about it, what are a few things that you could start doing today that would make a huge difference?

What are your key barriers?

What are some of the key barriers in your way? How can they be eliminated?

If you periodically evaluate where you are, it will help you get motivated and stay motivated because the periodic check-up will be your motivational "compass" and will help you stay pointed in the right direction.

WORK IT

This is the portion of the book when you begin to apply to your life what you just read. So let's get busy and WORKIT by answering the following questions! Let the pencil fly, and don't edit your answers, just write the first thoughts that come to mind.

EVALUATE WHERE YOU ARE

Evaluating where you are, how do you feel about your progress?

What is going well?

What are some obstacles you may face? What can you do to get around the obstacles?

____

____

____

____

What do you need improve?

____

____

____

____

What can you do differently?

____

____

____

____

What are three areas that you can target for improvement?

1. ______________________________________

____

____

2. ______________________________________

____

____

3. ______________________________________

Why did you set the goals to begin with?

ACTION LIST

Now that you have worked through these questions, what are three actions that you can take over the next 30 days that you can go back and track in a few months?

1.

2.

3.

Now write these action items in your calendar.

CHAPTER ELEVEN

FOUNDATION #10
LIVE A LIFE OF BALANCE

"Not life, but good life, is to be chiefly valued."
—SOCRATES

WHAT is the definition of success? Some people would define success as financial success like that of Donald Trump or Bill Gates. Some would define it as artistic success like that of that of Picasso. Some would define success as the serving lives of Martin Luther King Jr., or Mother Teresa. Most people would view a successful person as someone who has achieved a lot—written 35 books, broken all the sports records, started a successful company, climbed Mount Everest. Success can be viewed, however, in a different light, and that is the enviable state of living a life of balance. We have all read stories of "successful" actresses or actors who were famous and very wealthy, but were horrible parents and experienced several failed marriages. We have heard of successful business leaders who were phenomenally effective and results-oriented at work while failing miserably at home; divorced with broken families. These people seem happy on the surface and have all the trappings of success and fame. On the other hand we all know or have known great fathers and mothers and family members who couldn't hold down a good job and had little or no success in the business world.

The key, in my opinion, is to strive to live a life of balance. The idea is to be successful in all areas of your life because they all affect one another. If you have a happy home life, you probably will be a more productive worker at the office. If you have a level of fitness, you probably will be in a better frame of mind at work and at home because you will have more energy and be mentally sharper. It has a domino effect.

Living a life of balance will help you get motivated and stay motivated because it will help you in several ways:

- You will tend to be less frustrated because you will be making progress in each area of your life.
- When you are working on one area of your life, you can be more focused. You won't be worried about the other areas because you will already be making progress.
- You will feel good about your life overall.

BALANCE MYTHOLOGY

Before we go further and give you some tips about how to live a life of balance, we should talk about some myths I would like you to get out of your head. If you understand these up front, you will be less likely to get frustrated on your journey of seeking life balance.

Myth #1

Life will be or should be perfectly balanced. Forget this concept! There is no such thing as perfection and there is no such thing as perfect balance. I know, you are saying to yourself, "Yes, but I know a lady who had absolute perfect balance." (Martha Stewart?) Well, that is your perception. Believe me when I tell you that everyone on this planet struggles with this, and as we get busier and more tied to technology with computers and cell phones, it's getting crazier.

Myth #2

Once I am balanced I will be set. This is also very far from the truth; the reality is that balance is like the wheels on your car. You can get them balanced, but after some wear and tear and bumpy roads, you have to get them balanced again. So balance is something that has to be done over and over again in your life. It is a process.

Myth # 3

Balance is a goal that is achieved. The truth is that balance is a process that you go through each week and every month. Every week you are deciding where to spend time and what to spend it on. It is in those individual decisions that balance can be achieved.

Myth #4

I will always be balanced. Not true! There will be weeks where, due to a big project or initiative, you will have to spend much more time at work. There will be weeks when a family member is sick and you will have to spend more time at home. There will be weeks when you are sick and can't work out. So the target is to achieve balance, but you will be less frustrated if you understand that it will not always happen.

When you look at balance, you should try to concentrate on the following areas:

- Professional/Career
- Family Life/Friends
- Health and Fitness
- Spiritual
- Financial
- Intellectual

For each of these categories you should have both short and long term goals.

PROFESSIONAL/CAREER

This is an area that can have an impact on your life from a positive or negative viewpoint. Your professional/work life is key because in most cases, it is financing the rest of your life. If you think about it, your work is paying for the place you live, the car you drive, the food you eat. It is vital to spend time investing in and developing the skills that will help your career grow.

How do you balance work life with the rest of your life? It is not easy, and isn't getting any easier. Understand that you won't always be "in balance." There will be times when you are called on to make things happen, and you may have to kick up your efforts for a few weeks or even a few months. It can reduce your stress level to understand that there are times when you will be temporarily out of balance. When this happens, it is a good idea to get agreement from loved ones and friends that this will be the case for a little while. They will be forewarned and will know that it is temporary, which is fine. I was recently at a major theme park on vacation and saw a family with a father, mother, and three kids. Every time I saw that family throughout the day the father was on his cell phone. Now I am guessing, but I think his life was out of balance. He didn't have time to go on vacation! That to me was a sad example of what can happen when we don't strive for balance.

It could be that there was an emergency at the office or a crisis he was managing; however, I got the feeling that this man was just a person who is a workaholic and never will be in balance.

So what is the price we pay? What happens when we are utterly out of balance? At some point our motivation can be affected. The old saying "all work and no play makes Jack (and Jill) a dull boy/girl" certainly has some truth to it! The reality is that your tiny baby will only be a baby once. Your grandmother will only have a 100th birthday party once. Your son will only hit his first homerun once. There are so many special times that are missed and can't be replayed and are gone, never to return. The emotional hurt of family and friends is lasting.

I once had a job where I traveled 46 weeks during the year. My daughter was a toddler at the time and used to grab my leg and cry as I went out the door. Prying her little fingers from my leg and hugging her goodbye was painful. I would give her a hug and then say goodbye. It was the worst feeling in the world.

THE BIG QUESTION

The big question on balance between work and the rest of your life is simply that you have to decide where the line is drawn. I once interviewed for a sales position which was double my total compensation at the time. The only problem was that it required very heavy travel. I discussed it with my family and decided that it wasn't worth it. That is where we, as a family, drew the line.

You alone have to decide where the line is drawn. This is not an easy task because the line is always moving and work, as well as your life, is always in a state of change.

How can you tell if you lack balance? If you are already asking yourself that question— that may be a hint. If you work so much that it is negatively affecting your family, your health, your marriage, your friendships, your finances, you most likely have a problem with balance. That means you are working too hard.

You may want to try setting some guidelines for yourself on how many hours a week you are willing to put in, and try to stick to the maximum number. Many experts claim that you will work to fill the time available, and if you lessen the hours, you will get the same amount done. Secondly, when you set a guideline and stick to it, you will eliminate doubt (am I doing enough?) and guilt and the stress that goes along with it. Try it for a few weeks and see what happens.

Family Life/Friends

As a human being and as a member of the human tribe, you need to be connected to other people. As the old song goes, "What the world needs now is love, sweet love." As trite as that sounds, it's a basic human need. In order to be motivated and stay motivated, we need to be around people who we appreciate and people who appreciate us. I find that there are many people who don't give their family and friends enough attention because they are so busy. I find it easy to fall into this trap myself. The sad fact is we don't know how long we will be around and we don't know how long our friends and family will be around. I don't mean to be morbid, but this is a reality which can shape your perception about spending time with family.

Several years ago, my beloved grandfather passed away. He was more than just a grandfather, he was almost like a second father to me and he was a special person. We called him "Bigpop" This was certainly an appropriate name because he was big and he was full of life! Names like "grandfather" or "gramps" would have never have fit this giant energy-force of a man. I must confess to you that when I went to his funeral I wished that I had spent more time with him in the last year of his life. Why didn't I? I had led myself to believe I was too busy. It was six hours away; I didn't have enough days off, blah, blah, blah. The reality is I didn't plan for or make the time. I doubt there are many people at funerals that say, "I just wish I hadn't spent SO MUCH time with them."

The real issue with most of us is we don't plan and prioritize spending time with family and friends. It isn't part of our schedule. We get caught up in the day-to-day hustle and bustle of life. Spending time with friends and family becomes accidental instead of purposeful. I am proud to say I plan time with my teenage daughter. Borrowing a technique from Dr. Steven Covey (*The Seven Habits of Highly Effective People*) every month we have a "father/daughter" day. This is sacred time put aside when she and I plan and do something together.

It is the greatest decision we have ever made. As you may know, teens are not always easy to talk to. Every month we do something together. It may be seeing a movie (even a dumb one), miniature golf, bowling, or lunch. I allow her to choose the activity, and she really enjoys our time together. She will also remind me if we have missed that month! There is an amazing side effect of these outings; we somehow always end up talking. This is precious and rare time with a teenager. The second action I took is I bought a trampoline. This was also a great way for my daughter and me to spend time together. While we are jumping and goofing around, we are spending time together and having meaningful discussions.

My wife and I have been married for 24 years but we still have "dates." We plan time to go out to movies, dinner, or shows in order to spend quality time together as a couple.

Make the time for family and friends and actually plan it on your calendar. If you want to stay in touch with your best friend or your favorite cousin, write it in your calendar and then do it! The connection to family and friends will help you be more motivated. How can spending time with family and friends help you be motivated? Family and friends are already on your side, and they can help support you, encourage you, and give you love when you need that extra boost. That can be very motivating to know that you are part of a family that is behind you.

Physical/Health

I started out my career in retail, and I will never forget "Mr. B." He reminded me of a Jack Russell terrier, he was very small, very skinny, and was always wired. He drank six cups of coffee before 7 A.M. and smoked two packs of cigarettes a day. He never ate lunch and never stopped working. He was, in my mind, the picture of poor health and a heart attack waiting to happen. He was very stressed out and lost his temper quickly. I wonder how he is doing today? According to research, only 16% of the American population is on a regular workout program. That means that 84% of Americans are not! Recent research also indicates that 64% of all men and 42% of all women are classified as overweight! That means that most Americans get little or no exercise, and if you sit on any city street and observe people walking by, you will see the result. I know many people who don't make exercise part of their daily routine. We all have heard the excuses; "I don't have time" or "I can't afford to belong to a gym" or "I just got out of the habit".

We all end up so busy that if we don't work out, at some point our body starts to betray us. We slow down, feel bad, don't have energy like we used to have. My wife's doctor said,

"All my patients that are sick in their 50's are a result of what they did or didn't do in their 30's and 40's." As the old saying goes, "You reap what you sow."

But there is very good news, there is a fountain of youth just ready and waiting for you to take a drink, and that is exercise!!!! Exercise will provide more energy, more confidence, higher self-esteem, mental alertness, and you will be more motivated. Here is the formula:

PH= > E > M

The formula is that physical health equals increased energy and increased motivation. Think about it, when are you most motivated? When you have the most energy! When are you the least motivated? When you have the least energy and you are tired. That is when you are most likely to be "down." If you want to maximize motivation, you must maximize your body and your overall health.

I have found two keys to maximum health: a reasonable dietary plan and a workout plan that is reasonable and will help me maintain consistency.

THE CABBAGE DIET

I am very concerned that across America there are people who are starting plans that are doomed to failure because the plans are so CRAZY. One day I was talking to someone in the office and they said they were excited because they were starting a new diet. Wanting to be supportive, I asked them about it. They told me excitedly about the "soup diet" where each day all they would eat was soup made from certain vegetables, for days. This form of dieting is horrible because the person on the diet ultimately gets so hungry they go off the diet and fail. Then the next time they go on a diet (another crazy one) they say to themselves, "Well, I failed the last time." A popular diet recently advertised "Lose ten pounds in two days!" If that isn't insane, I don't know what is! In order to stay motivated, I believe you must find an eating plan which is reasonable; something that a normal person can stick with and get results over time.

When exercising, I have found two keys to success that work for me. I have to keep going back to the reason I am working out (Principle #1—Have a Purpose for What You Do) In other words, why are you working out? To lose weight? To live a long, healthy life free of disease? To increase the quality of your life? To attract a mate? The reasons have to be your reasons, and the more detailed and specific you are, the better.

The second key for me is it has to be a form of exercise that I enjoy. If I don't enjoy it, forget about it! I know this sounds so blatantly obvious, but there are lots of folks who don't enjoy exercising and think it should be a chore. Not true! I hate running on a treadmill. For me, it is as boring as watching grass grow. So I have tried to find forms of exercise that I really enjoy. I hate aerobics, but I love kickboxing, I can't stand yoga, but I love Pilates. I don't care for running but I love jumping rope. My wife, for example, doesn't really like the treadmill, but because she loves being outside, she will run for an hour. The key is to find the form of exercise that works for you, and if you don't like it, don't do it! So make your workouts more enjoyable and start having fun!

Spiritual

I want to start off by saying that "spiritual" has a very broad meaning; it can mean any traditional religious belief or could mean the act of studying, reading, or meditating. I would prefer to leave the definition of "spiritual" up to you. My definition of spiritual is something that renews me, refreshes my spirit, and makes me feel whole. I believe that the reason people start feeling burnt out or dispirited is they neglect their spiritual side.

It is very easy in today's world of speed and urgency, to not take the time to slow down, reflect, think, meditate, or pray. My wife and I were enjoying a long weekend at Rehoboth Beach, Delaware. The weather was great, the beach was beautiful, and I could feel the ocean air taking the stress away. I was walking down the boardwalk and saw a woman about 35 sitting on a bench looking out at the ocean. She also had a device in her hand and was clicking through and answering e-mail. I had to laugh. What is the point? Why go away if you can't get away?

Taking the time to renew your spirit, making the time to renew yourself will make an impact and have a significant effect on the rest of your life. You will be calmer, more focused, and more motivated!

Financial

I am constantly amazed and amused at the credit card companies and how they have been able to lure people into more and more and more debt. When I first graduated from college, I was inundated with offers from credit card companies offering me all sorts of cards even before I had a job! Today, I am sure there is not one day that goes by that I don't get a credit card offer. Every store that I visit, the last thing the cashier says before they ring your sale is, "Would you like one of our credit cards?"

I have heard about married couples earning average incomes that have credit card debt that is half of their yearly income. They end up having to get a loan to pay their loan! This is, in my mind, an insane way to exist. That is why financial balance is so very important. There are several reasons why financial balance is beneficial:

- You will save a ton of money by eliminating high-interest credit cards.
- A great credit rating allows you to take advantage of opportunities such as buying houses or cars.
- This book is about how to get motivated and stay motivated; however, and here is the bottom line, when your finances are in order, you have peace of mind and can ease anxiety and stress, therefore being more motivated.
- If the stress is eliminated, you can spend your energies on other areas like goal-setting and defining your purpose.

When we were a young married couple, we were expecting our first child. Unfortunately, in the eighth month, my wife developed complications and was hospitalized. She was in the hospital for one month. When she was discharged, you can imagine the bill that was handed to me. It weighed about five pounds. We had insurance, but the insurance was an 80/20 plan. That meant that we were responsible for 20%, which came to a whopping $16,000.00! I almost fainted. Of course I didn't have that kind of money. I arranged a payment plan with the hospital, doctors, and many others. Technically at that time we could have easily and legitimately declared bankruptcy, but my wife and I decided we would not take that road, partly from stubborn pride and partly with an eye toward the long-term. It took a very long time, but we finally paid it back, every penny. I can tell you that it was a very stressful and demoralizing time, having people call you to say that you were not "paying fast enough" and applying pressure tactics. To use a famous line from *A Tale of Two Cities*, "It was the best of times, it was the worst of times." The worst of times because of the financial pressure and the best because of our daughter's birth. But we made it through with dogged determination and backbone.

If you haven't already, it's a good idea to gain financial literacy so that you can use money for what it is, a tool. It would also help you to understand what financial balance looks like.

One of the problems with our society today is that none of us want to wait. We want the big house now, the big, expensive car now and some of us are not willing to "pay our dues." The credit card and finance companies encourage this, foster it, and paint the picture that creates the hunger for instant gratification. They constantly raise the limits of what people can spend on cars, loans, and mortgages. They make it so easy to get approval and to spend it. This is, in many ways, a factor for lower motivation.

If you can maintain a financial balance, you will feel more confident, more competent and more motivated on a day-to-day basis.

Intellectual

If you have been out of school for a while, I have a question: Are you still learning? Still studying? Still growing intellectually? Do you still have a thirst for new information?

As mentioned in Principle #3, you need to be a non-stop, continuous learning machine.

What do you know? From a professional and personal learning standpoint, what do you need to know? What knowledge and information will you need in order to get to the "next level"? Go out and find this information on the internet, in the library, or in a seminar. The people who I believe will have the competitive edge in the future will be the people who keep upgrading their knowledge and skills, especially when there are other people who aren't. I suggest developing a customized "learning plan" in order to evaluate where you are and where you need to be. Then determine how you are going to get this information. If you don't know what it is you need to work on, here are some sources you may want to consider:

A Mentor

Your mentor can often see areas that need improvement that you cannot perceive. This is when an honest, straightforward mentor can be a big help.

Assessments

There are tons of written and web-based assessments on nearly any topic that you can locate and complete that will give you results that are measurable and specific.

Colleagues

Ask a trusted co-worker to give you feedback on areas that they see for improvement. As a word of caution, make sure that you are in the right frame of mind when you receive feedback. This is to help you, so don't get defensive.

Friends/family

If you have a smart, perceptive family member who can give you feedback, ask them for help. Just make sure you select the right family; remember who is truly in your corner. I have had the privilege of having been married for many years and my wife gives great advice that is both perceptive and clear. She also has the advantage of being objective, which is in part due to the fact that she is not involved with my professional life and can see the forest when I can only see the trees at times.

So decide on a plan to grow, and you will be amazed at the results.

If you are feeling stagnant or unmotivated, it can be caused by a few factors:

Burnout

Working too hard on too many things for too long.

Lack of Goals

Chasing the pot at the end of the rainbow and having no idea why you are doing it.

Wrong work

Doing the wrong work with the wrong company and the wrong people. (If this is the case, you know it in your gut.)

Lack of balance

Concentrating all your efforts on one area of your life at the expense of all others.

If you face any of these situations, take some time to stop and evaluate what is going on. Take the bull by the horns and start taking action! Don't wait, don't procrastinate or hesitate—you have a brand new life to create!

WORK IT

This is the portion of the book when you begin to apply to your life what you just read. So let's get busy and WORKIT by answering the following questions! Let the pencil fly, and don't edit your answers, just write the first thoughts that come to mind.

A LIFE OF BALANCE

Of the areas of professional/career, family/friends, physical/health, spiritual, financial, intellectual, which areas are your strengths right now?

____

____

____

____

What areas are the ones that you would like to improve?

____

____

____

____

What specific steps can you take to start improving them tomorrow?

____

____

Why are these areas that you have neglected?

What impact would improving this area have?

What do you need to learn?

What would help you personally? What would help you professionally?

ACTION LIST

Now that you have worked through these questions, what are three actions that you can take over the next 30 days that will bring you closer to living a life of balance?

1.

2.

3.

Now write these action items on your calendar.

CHAPTER 12

A BRAND NEW YOU!

Be willing to reinvent yourself; because if Cher and Madonna can do it, you can!

—NWAHS ELYOD

AS the lion in the Wizard of Oz said, "Courage!" (Dan Rather later briefly adopted this, but give him credit for trying something new!) Why do I mention courage? Because it takes courage to be willing to create a brand new you; it takes courage to reinvent yourself because you don't know how it will work out! Secondly, you may face ridicule and failure. You may stumble and fall. SO WHAT! Do it anyway and full speed ahead. Hell with them all; man the torpedoes. This is your life, Bucko.

I want you to imagine that you could jump into a time machine and become invisible. You travel back in time and you are able to see yourself and spy on the ten-year-old you. What do you see? What did you dream of doing? What did you dream of being before society told you that you couldn't? An astronaut? A professional ball player? A famous artist? A millionaire? An actor? The President of the United States?

Somewhere along the way, we all have stumbled. We have made wrong decisions, bad choices and have made mistakes. Sometimes those mistakes have puzzled us. We say, "Why did we do that?" or "What in the world was I thinking?" We all make errors in judgment at times. This can be frustrating and sometimes you look back at your past with regret at the actions that you took or did not take. This can be very destructive if you dwell on it too long. The only useful exercise in looking back at the past is for fond memories and for learning what you can do differently or better in the future.

Tomorrow the sun will rise above the horizon and it will be a brand new day. You will wake up and get out of bed to an opportunity. You and your super smart, incredibly capable brain will look at the world and make a decision. You will decide to become a new you. You will be motivated, and you will stay motivated, and the people in your life will notice a difference. Your life will become a motivation for others.

In order to be this new person, you will have committed to some key ideas:

FOUNDATION #1

Have a purpose for what you do. You will get up every day, knowing why you are on this planet and reason why you do what you do.

FOUNDATION #2

Have a passion for what you do. You will be excited because you will be doing the work that you are passionate about, and you will be excited about what you do.

FOUNDATION #3

Be a continuous non-stop learning machine. You will be a committed learner who is always reading, studying, and learning. You have a spark in your eye and a bounce in your step knowing that you are growing.

FOUNDATION #4

Be a mentor and have a mentor. You will be a mentor to someone, your guidance and direction is having a big impact on their life. You also have a mentor who is really helping you grow and look at the world with a different perspective.

FOUNDATION #5

Know what gets you stimulated and keeps you motivated. You know exactly what keeps you stimulated and motivated. On the occasional "tough day," you will have tools that will get you back in the proper frame of mind.

FOUNDATION #6

Reward yourself for achieving. You will be motivated because as you achieve your goals along the way, you will reward yourself for achieving. Because you see the tangible fruits of your efforts, you are constantly achieving more.

FOUNDATION #7

Practice long-term thinking. You make decisions about your professional and personal life based on a view of the future or long-term thinking. This keeps you focused and motivated because you have a long-term view.

FOUNDATION #8

Keep growing and achieving. You are a person who understands the proposition that if you don't go forward, you are going backward. Stagnation is not an option. You are always growing because you believe in this principle, and it keeps you driven.

FOUNDATION #9

Periodically evaluate where you are. You take the time on occasion to stop and look at all of your goals that you have set, to evaluate where you are. This keeps you motivated and "fired up" because you are regularly giving yourself a report on your own progress. You are your own board of directors and you are doing well.

FOUNDATION #10

Live a life of balance. You are a person who is in balance. No part of your life is "neglected." You know that you are balanced and you feel good about it.

So that is it. We have reached the end of the story and the grand finale, if you like. It is the beginning of your story. It is now entirely up to you. I can lead you to water, but it is up to you to drink it. So get going, time is passing as we speak. Go out there and create a life that will be an inspiration to others! *Carpe Diem*!

I hope you enjoyed this book.

Shawn Doyle is a motivational speaker, author, trainer, consultant, and business coach. He is available to provide the following services:

Speaking at your next meeting
Training on sales, motivation, or leadership
Custom training
Executive coaching
Life coaching
Sales coaching

If you would like to contact Shawn with questions or comments, send Shawn an e mail at SLDoyle1@aol.com.

Visit our website for free articles and other resources:
www.sldoyle.com

ABOUT SHAWN DOYLE

SHAWN Doyle is a learning and development professional who has a passion for human potential. He has an avid belief in the concept of lifelong learning. For the last 20 years, Shawn has spent his time developing and implementing training programs on team building, communication, creativity, and leadership. This has been in order to help people become more effective in the workplace and in their lives. Some clients include Pfizer, Comcast, Charter Media, IBM, Kraft, Microsoft, the Marines, the Ladders, and Los Alamos National Defense Laboratory.